STUDY GUIDE
TO ACCOMPANY
SOCIAL PSYCHOLOGY
Ninth Edition

David G. Myers
Hope College

Prepared by

Martin Bolt
Calvin College

McGraw Hill

Boston   Burr Ridge, IL   Dubuque, IA   Madison, WI   New York   San Francisco   St. Louis
Bangkok   Bogotá   Caracas   Kuala Lumpur   Lisbon   London   Madrid   Mexico City
Milan   Montreal   New Delhi   Santiago   Seoul   Singapore   Sydney   Taipei   Toronto

The *McGraw·Hill* Companies

McGraw-Hill Higher Education

Study Guide to accompany
SOCIAL PSYCHOLOGY
David G. Myers

Published by McGraw-Hill Higher Education, an imprint of The McGraw-Hill Companies, Inc.,
1221 Avenue of the Americas, New York, NY 10020. Copyright © 2008, 2005, 2002, 1999, 1996, 1993, 1990,
1987, 1983 by The McGraw-Hill Companies, Inc. All rights reserved. Printed in the United States of
America. No part of this publication may be reproduced or distributed in any form or by any means,
or stored in a database or retrieval system, without prior written consent of The McGraw-Hill Companies, Inc.,
including, but not limited to, in any network or other electronic storage or transmission, or broadcast for
distance learning.

2 3 4 5 6 7 8 9 0 BKM/BKM 0 9 8 7

ISBN 978-0-07-326538-4
MHID 0-07-326538-1

www.mhhe.com

CONTENTS

INTRODUCTION: HOW TO USE THIS STUDY GUIDE

This study guide is designed to help you master the material presented in David G. Myers' *Social Psychology*, ninth edition. It also tests your comprehension of text material and provides a review for class examination. Each chapter in the study guide corresponds to a text chapter and is organized into the following sections:

Chapter Objectives. This opening section highlights the chapter's learning goals and thus provides a basis for self-evaluation. Because the objectives constitute an overview of the chapter's major ideas and organization, you may also want to review them before reading the chapter.

Chapter Review. This fill-in-the-blank summary reviews the chapter's major ideas: the subheadings parallel those in the text. You may choose either to fill in the blanks section by section after you have read the respective text material, or to wait until you have finished the entire chapter. (The answers are in the Answer Key at the end of each chapter.) This review also provides a quick refresher quiz just before a class examination.

Matching Terms. This exercise provides a list of concepts you should be familiar with after studying the chapter. Close attention to the definitions provided in the textbook's margin will promote your mastery of the chapter's key terms.

True-False Review. These items, along with the multiple-choice questions that follow, offer a means of assessing your progress in mastering the chapter's content. They also provide additional review of some of the chapter's major ideas.

Multiple-Choice Practice Test. Multiple-choice items are commonly used in classroom tests and you may want to wait until you feel you are adequately prepared to take a regular examination before completing this section as practice. Most of the items assess your knowledge of the chapter's basic content. A few challenge you to go beyond the information presented in the text and to apply it to new problems and situations.

Short Essay Questions. Your ability to answer these questions indicates whether you have mastered the chapter objectives.

Answer Key. This section gives the answers to the Chapter Review, Matching Terms, True-False, and Multiple-Choice exercises. Checking your answers will reveal sections of the chapter that may require additional review.

CHAPTER 1

INTRODUCING SOCIAL PSYCHOLOGY

CHAPTER OBJECTIVES

After completing your study of this chapter you should be able to:

1. Define social psychology and give examples of the discipline's central concerns.

2. Identify social psychology's overarching themes.

3. Indicate how the personal values of social psychologists penetrate their work.

4. Discuss the nature and the implications of the "hindsight bias" for social psychology.

5. Explain the general nature and purpose of a theory.

6. Describe two major research methods used in social psychology and state the advantages and disadvantages of each.

7. Identify ethical standards that govern social-psychological research.

CHAPTER REVIEW

Supply the words necessary to complete each of the following statements.

WHAT IS SOCIAL PSYCHOLOGY?

1. Social psychology is the ___scientific___ study of how people think about, ___influence___, and relate to one another. It is still a ___young___ discipline with the first social psychology experiments being reported barely more than a ___century___ ago.

SOCIAL PSYCHOLOGY'S BIG IDEAS

2. We _construct_ our social reality. Our social _intuitions_ are often powerful but sometimes _perilous_.

3. Social _influences_ shape our behavior. In addition, personal attitudes and _personality_ shape behavior.

4. Social behavior is also _biological_ behavior. Social psychology's principles are _applicable_ in _everyday_ life.

5. As but one _perspective_ on human existence, psychological science does not seek to engage life's _ultimate_ questions.

SOCIAL PSYCHOLOGY AND HUMAN VALUES

6. Social psychologists' personal _values_ penetrate their work in obvious ways such as their _choice_ of research topics.

7. In addition, awareness is growing that science is not as purely _objective_ as commonly thought. The scientists' _preconceptions_ control their interpretations and _values_ are hidden in the concepts and labels of social psychology.

I KNEW IT ALL ALONG: IS SOCIAL PSYCHOLOGY SIMPLY COMMON SENSE?

8. The _hindsight_ bias is the tendency to exaggerate one's ability to have foreseen how something turned out after learning the outcome; it may explain why social psychology's findings often seem like _common sense_.

RESEARCH METHODS: HOW WE DO SOCIAL PSYCHOLOGY

9. Social psychologists organize their ideas and findings into _theories_ that both explain and _predict_ observed events.

10. Most social psychological research is conducted either in the _laboratory_ or in the _field_ and is either _correlational_ or _experimental_.

11. The great strength of correlational research is that it tends to occur in _real-world_ settings where it can examine important factors that cannot be _manipulated_ in the laboratory. Correlational research can tell us whether two variables are associated but cannot provide _cause & effect_ explanations.

12. Survey researchers obtain a representative group by taking a _random sample_ in which every person in the total group has an equal chance of being chosen to participate. About _1,200_ randomly selected participants will enable the researcher to be 95 percent confident of describing the entire population within an error margin of 3 percent or less. Four potentially biasing influences on surveys are _unrepresentative_ samples, the _order_ in which questions are asked, the _response_ options, and the _wording_ of the questions.

13. Two essential ingredients of every social-psychological experiment are

    control and _random_ assignment.

    Researchers often walk a tightrope in designing experiments that will be involving yet

    ethical.

MATCHING TERMS

Write the letter of the term on the right before the appropriate number on the left.

_j._ 1. A cue in an experiment that tells the participant what behavior is expected.
demand characteristic

a. social representations

_c._ 2. The study of the naturally occurring relationships among variables.
correlational research

b. random assignment

_m._ 3. An integrated set of principles that explain and predict observed events.
Theory

c. correlational research

_a._ 4. Socially shared beliefs that help us make sense of our world.
Social representations

d. mundane realism

_h._ 5. Research done in natural, real-life settings outside the laboratory.
Field Research

e. random sample

_b._ 6. Placing participants in an experiment such that each has an equal chance of being in a given condition.
Random Assignment

f. experimental realism

_k._ 7. Research participants must be told enough to enable them to choose whether they wish to participate.
Informed Consent

g. hindsight bias

_i._ 8. Seeks clues to cause-effect relationships by manipulating one or more factors while controlling others.
Experimental Research

h. field research

_e._ 9. Every person in the group has had an equal chance of being chosen to participate in a study.
Random Sample

i. experimental research

_g._ 10. The tendency to exaggerate one's ability to have foreseen how something turned out, after learning the outcome.
Hindsight Bias

j. demand characteristic

_d._ 11. Extent to which an experiment is superficially similar to everyday situations.
Mundane realism

k. informed consent

_f._ 12. Extent to which an experiment absorbs and involves its participants.
Experimental Realism

l. culture

_l._ 13. Enduring behaviors and ideas shared by a large group of people and transmitted from one generation to the next.
Culture

m. theory

4

TRUE-FALSE REVIEW

Circle T if the statement is true and F if it is false.

T (F) 1. The first social psychology experiments were reported in the 1930s.

T (F) 2. The first social psychology text was published in 1898.

T (F) 3. Contemporary social psychology downplays the biological foundations of behavior.

(T) (F) 4. In comparison to social psychologists, personality psychologists have a special concern for the similarities between individuals.

(T) F 5. Thinking, memory, and attitudes operate on two levels—one conscious and deliberate, the other unconscious and automatic.

T (F) 6. Social neuroscientists aim to reduce complex social behaviors to simple neural or molecular mechanisms.

(T) F 7. Social representations are our most important but least examined convictions.

(T) F 8. A study of the Princeton-Dartmouth football game showed how our opinions control our interpretations.

T (F) 9. The "I-Knew-It-All-Along" phenomenon provides one example of "dual processing."

(T) F 10. Social psychologists have investigated how values are formed and how they can be changed.

T (F) 11. Hidden value judgments are more common in psychology than in sociology.

T (F) 12. Random assignment is an important feature of well-done surveys.

(T) F 13. A total of 1200 randomly selected participants will enable a survey researcher to be 95 percent confident of describing the entire population of a country with an error margin of 3 percent or less.

(T) F 14. The order in which questions are asked can influence respondents' answers in a survey.

(T) F 15. There are at least three possible explanations for every correlational finding.

(T) F 16. Contemporary social psychology recognizes the importance of our intuitions in understanding social behavior.

(T) F 17. The experimental method enables researchers to answer questions about causal relationships.

T (F) 18. The correlational method is used in about one-half of social-psychological research studies.

(T) F 19. Demand characteristics are cues in an experiment that tell the participant what behavior is expected.

T (F) 20. An experiment has mundane realism if it absorbs and involves its participants.

(T) F 21. One ethical principle advocated by the American Psychological Association is that investigators treat information about the individual research participants confidentially.

T (F) 22. Theories are most frequently discarded because they have been falsified.

(T) F 23. A good theory makes clear predictions that can be used to confirm or to modify the theory.

T (F) 24. The findings of social psychology typically prove that common sense ideas are wrong.

(T) F 25. Hindsight bias is conducive to arrogance—an overestimation of our own intellectual powers.

MULTIPLE-CHOICE PRACTICE TEST

Circle the correct letter.

1. Social psychology is the scientific study of how people ___think about___, ___influence___, and ___relate to___ one another.

    a. understand, feel about, act toward
    b. perceive, think about, act toward
    (c.) think about, influence, relate to
    d. observe, influence, conflict with

2. Social psychology began to emerge as the vibrant field it is today during

    a. the depression of the early 1930s when researchers examined the effects of deprivation on aggression and altruism
    b. World War I when psychologists conducted studies of social conflict and cooperation
    (c.) World War II when researchers contributed studies of persuasion and soldier morale
    d. the Korean War when psychologists examined the effects of brainwashing on prisoners of war

3. The text uses the folktale *Cinderella* to illustrate the power of

   a. human imagination
   b. situations
   c. social status
   d. narrative

4. Researchers use the term *dual processing* to refer to the fact that

   a. thinking occurs on both conscious and unconscious levels
   b. nature and nurture determine social behavior
   c. love and hate characterize our social interactions
   d. past and present situations determine our behavior

5. According to the text, social psychology is a science that studies the impact of our

   a. situations
   b. family background
   c. aptitudes
   d. unconscious motives

6. Social psychology addresses all of the following questions <u>except</u> which one?

   a. How do our social intuitions sometimes deceive us?
   b. How is our social behavior shaped by our biology?
   c. What is our ultimate destiny?
   d. What are the causes of love and hate?

7. The text states that as a scientific discipline, social psychology

   a. is superior to those disciplines that assume a more subjective approach to the study of human nature
   b. can assist in explaining the meaning of life
   c. gives us a method for asking and answering some important questions
   d. offers explanations for human nature that often contradict the claims of other disciplines

8. Most social-psychological research is conducted either in the field or in the
   _laboratory_____ and is either correlational or _experimental_____.

   a. clinic; survey
   b. laboratory; experimental
   c. laboratory; survey
   d. clinic; experimental

9. Survey researchers obtain a representative group

   a. through random assignment
   b. by selecting at least 2000 respondents to be interviewed
   c. by taking a random sample
   d. through either telephone books or automobile registrations

10. The great strength of _correlational_ research _____ is that it tends to occur in real-world settings where it can examine questions regarding important factors such as race, sex, and social status.

   a. correlational research
   b. field experimentation
   c. laboratory experimentation
   d. quasi-experimentation

11. Which of the following distinguishes the correlational method from experimentation?

   a. The correlational method uses a smaller group of subjects
   b The correlational method enables researchers to study social attitudes
   c. With the correlational method no attempt is made to systematically manipulate one or more factors
   d. The findings from the correlational method are more likely to be contaminated by the experimenter's values

12. To determine whether changing one variable (such as education) produces changes in another (such as income), we need to conduct _experimental_ research.

   a. survey
   b. correlational
   c. experimental
   d. statistical

13. "Random assignment" means that each person taking part in an experiment must
   a. have an equal chance of being in a given condition in the experiment
   b. be assigned to all the conditions of the experimental treatment
   c. be randomly selected from the larger population
   d. be given random responses to the experimenter's questions

14. An experiment has mundane realism if

   a. the experimental task is similar to tasks in everyday life
   b. it involves and absorbs people
   c. it is conducted in the field
   d. the experimenter deceives subjects

15. The experimental factor that the experimenter manipulates is called the _experimental_ variable.

   a. dependent
   b. control
   c. independent
   d. experimental

16. In an experiment, the variable being measured is called the _dependent_ variable.

   a. control
   b. independent
   c. experimental
   d. dependent

17. The experimental method is used in about _____three-fourths_____ of all social-psychological research studies.

    a. one-fourth   c. three-fourths
    b. one-half   d. nine-tenths

18. Random assignment is necessary to

    a. insure mundane realism
    b. insure informed consent
    c. rule out preexisting differences between subjects in different experimental conditions
    d. avoid the naturalistic fallacy

19. Which of the following is false according to the text?

    a. Experimenters standardize their instructions to subjects to minimize demand characteristics
    b. The American Psychological Association has developed a number of ethical principles to guide investigators
    c. Informed consent is an important ethical principle to be followed in conducting research
    d. Deception should never be used in conducting research

20. Hypotheses are best characterized as

    a. axioms   c. predictions
    b. principles   d. conclusions

21. According to the text, _____the hindsight bias_____ tends to make people overconfident about the validity of their judgments and predictions.

    a. the fundamental attribution error   c. the naturalistic fallacy
    b. illusory correlation   d. the hindsight bias

22. In an experimental study of the effects of failure on self-esteem, self-esteem is the

    a. control condition   c. dependent variable
    b. independent variable   d. experimental condition

23. Widely held ideas and values that we take for granted and that help us make sense of our world are called

    a. pluralistic assumptions   c. social heuristics
    b. cultural traditions   d. social representations

24. The author of the text suggests that adjectives such as *self-actualized*, *mature*, and *well-adjusted* demonstrate

    a. how psychological concepts have hidden values
    b. how psychological concepts are individualistic
    c. an inordinate concern with mental health
    d. how personality psychologists are more influential than social psychologists

25. According to the text, the fact that human thinking always involves interpretation

    a. provides a valid reason for dismissing science
    b. is precisely why we need scientific analysis
    c. is a reason for preferring experimental over correlational research
    d. has been more frequently recognized by those in the sciences than by those in the humanities

26. How prior opinions control interpretations is illustrated by

    a. Hastorf and Cantril's study of reactions to the Princeton-Dartmouth football game
    b. Slovic and Fischhoff's study of the "I-Knew-It-All-Along" phenomenon
    c. the *Literary Digest*'s erroneous prediction of the winner of the 1936 presidential election
    d. Bachman and O'Malley's study of the relationship between self-esteem and achievement

27. Researchers at the University of Texas who sought to quantify students' social behaviors by having them wear microcassette recorders and microphones reported that almost _____ percent of their students' time was spent talking.

    a. 10
    b. 20
    c. 30
    d. 40

28. Social psychology's overarching themes include the idea that

    a. social development is a lifelong process
    b. social behaviors can be reduced to simple neural or molecular mechanisms
    c. our social intuitions are usually wrong
    d. personal attitudes and dispositions shape behavior

29. Several psychologists have challenged the idea that

    a. high self-esteem produces academic achievement
    b. the ingredients of loneliness are the same in different cultures
    c. parental education predicts children's achievement
    d. televised violence is a cause of children's aggressive behavior

30. A researcher who studies how an exchange of gifts or favors enabled our ancestors to survive and reproduce most clearly reflects the concerns of

    a. biological economics
    b. psychoanalysis
    c. evolutionary psychology
    d. social theology

31. The close friends and relatives of suicide victims sometimes blame themselves for failing to have foreseen the signs of desperation in their lost friend or family member. This self-blame provides an example of

    a. a social representation
    b. dual processing
    c. mundane realism
    d. the hindsight bias

32. You would like to know the relationship between the number of psychology courses people take and these people's interpersonal sensitivity. You survey college students to determine how much psychology they have taken and then have them complete a test of social sensitivity. Finally you plot the relationship. This is an example of

    a. a laboratory experiment
    b. a field experiment
    c. a correlational study
    d. participant observation

33. The telephone company wants to survey its 100,000 customers. Four proposals for sampling the customers are being considered. Which would you recommend?

    a. Interview every 75th person listed in the telephone directory
    b. Mail a questionnaire to all 100,000 customers and assume at least 1200 will respond
    c. Interview the people in every 50th residence from a postal listing of all addresses
    d. Iinterview those 1,000 persons with the highest phone bills

34. A research psychologist manipulates the level of fear in human subjects in the laboratory and then examines what effect the different levels of fear have on the subjects' reaction times. In this study, reaction time is the _____ variable.

    a. dependent
    b. correlational
    c. independent
    d. experimental

35. In conducting a study of conformity, the experimenters decide to tape-record the instructions that are to be presented to all subjects. Their decision is most likely an attempt to minimize the effect of

    a. hindsight bias
    b. mundane realism
    c. social expectations
    d. demand characteristics

36. A researcher is attempting to identify the brain area that enables us to experience empathy for victims of social injustice. Her work clearly reflects the concerns of

    a. biological sociology
    b. altruistic biology
    c. evolutionary psychology
    d. social neuroscience

11

37. Which of the following research methods would be most effective in demonstrating that the presence of others improves our performance of a task?

a. an experiment
b. a correlational study
c. a survey
d. a field study

38. Which of the following techniques would be the most effective way of investigating the relationship between the political preferences and the age of American citizens?

a. an experiment
b. a case study
c. a correlational study
d. participant observation

39. A negative correlation between degree of wealth and the likelihood of being involved in criminal activity would indicate that

a. poverty makes people more likely to commit a crime
b. the poor are more likely to be involved in criminal activity than are the wealthy
c. being involved in criminal activity usually prevents people from accumulating wealth
d. all these are necessarily true

40. In a research study investigating the effects of stress on the desire to affiliate, half of the participants complete an easy test of mental ability and half complete a difficult test. What technique should the investigators use to ensure that any post-test differences in the group's desire to affiliate actually result from the differences in test difficulty?

a. random sampling
b. random assignment
c. replication
d. correlational measurement

SHORT ESSAY QUESTIONS

Answer the following questions in the space provided.

1. Define *social psychology*.

The scientific study of how people think about influence and relate to one another.

2. Briefly describe three of social psychology's big lessons or overarching themes.

- How we construe our social worlds.
- How our social intuitions guide and sometimes deceive us.
- How social psychology's principles apply to our everyday lives.

    1.) We construe our social worlds.

    2) social intuitions guide + deceive us

    3. social psych principles apply to our everyday lives.

3. Briefly explain social psychology's connection to everyday life.

It is all about our lives, beliefs, relationships. Everyday we deal with social psychology. It guides our thinking and acting how we perceive the world and the people in it as well as ourselves.

4. Briefly describe three ways in which the personal values of social psychologists penetrate their work.

Defining the Good Life; Abraham Maslow was known for descriptions of "self-actualized" people. Descriptions of self-actualized personalities: spontaneous, autonomous + mystical were characteristics of Maslow's own personal values.

    1.) Choice of research topics

    2) types of people attracted to various fields of study

    3.) Hidden assumptions when forming concepts, choosing labels, + giving advice.

5. What is the "I-Knew-It-All-Along" phenomenon? What are its implications for social psychology? *The tendency to exaggerate, after learning an outcome, one's ability to have foreseen how something turned out.*

6. Describe two important functions of a theory.

   Summarize and explaining facts
   1) Effectively summarizes a wide range of observations
   2) Makes clear predictions

7. Describe the differences between a correlational study and an experimental study.

   In a correlational study you ask whether two or more factors are naturally associated
   In a experimental study you manipulate some factor to see if it effects the other.

8. What ethical problems do social psychologists encounter in conducting research? How have these problems been addressed?

Chapter Review

1. scientific
   influence
   young
   century

2. construct
   intuitions
   perilous

3. influences
   dispositions

4. biological
   applicable
   everyday

5. perspective
   ultimate

6. values
   choice

7. objective
   preconceptions
   values

8. hindsight
   common sense

9. theories
   predict

10. laboratory
    field
    correlational
    experimental

11. real-world
    manipulated
    cause-effect

12. random sample
    1200
    unrepresentative
    order
    response
    wording

13. control
    random
    ethical

Matching Terms

1. j
2. c
3. m
4. a
5. h
6. b

7. k
8. i
9. e
10 g
11. d
12 f
13. 1

True-False Review

1.	F	14.	T
2.	F	15.	T
3.	F	16.	T
4.	F	17.	T
5.	T	18.	F
6.	F	19.	T
7.	T	20.	F
8.	T	21.	T
9.	F	22.	F
10.	T	23.	T
11.	F	24.	F
12.	F	25.	T
13.	T		

Multiple-Choice Practice Test

1.	c	21.	d
2.	c	22.	c
3.	b	23.	d
4.	a	24.	a
5.	a	25.	b
6.	c	26.	a
7.	c	27.	c
8.	b	28.	d
9.	c	29.	a
10.	a	30.	c
11.	c	31.	d
12.	c	32.	c
13.	a	33.	a
14.	a	34.	a
15.	c	35.	d
16.	d	36.	d
17.	c	37.	a
18.	c	38.	c
19.	d	39.	b
20.	c	40.	b

CHAPTER 2

THE SELF IN A SOCIAL WORLD

CHAPTER OBJECTIVES

After completing your study of this chapter you should be able to:

1. Describe the nature of the self-concept and discuss how our beliefs about ourselves influence our thoughts and actions.

2. Describe the factors that shape our self-concepts.

3. Discuss research findings regarding the accuracy of our self-knowledge.

4. Describe the controversy surrounding the value of high self-esteem.

5. Define self-efficacy and explain its relationship to behavior.

6. Give several examples of self-serving bias and discuss why people perceive themselves in self-enhancing ways.

7. Show how tactics of impression management may lead to false modesty or self-defeating behavior.

CHAPTER REVIEW

Supply the words necessary to complete each of the following statements.

SPOTLIGHTS AND ILLUSIONS
1. Our tendency to believe that others are paying more attention to us than they are is called the _Spotlight_ effect. Our tendency to believe that our emotions are more obvious than they are is the illusion of _transparency_.

SELF-CONCEPT: WHO AM I?
2. Our sense of _self_ helps organize our thoughts and actions. The self-_reference_ effect refers to the tendency to remember well information

related to oneself. The elements of our self-concept include the specific self-___schema___ that guide our processing of self-relevant information and the ___possible___ selves that we dream of or dread.

3. Multiple influences shape the self including the ___roles___ we play, the social identities we form, the social ___comparisons___ we make, our experiences of success and failure, other people's ___judgments___, and the surrounding ___culture___.

4. Some people, especially in industrialized Western cultures, value ___individualism___ (giving priority to one's own goals) and nurture an ___independent___ self. Others, for example in Asian and African cultures, place greater value on ___collectivism___ (giving priority to the goals of one's group) and nurture an ___interdependent___ self. These contrasting ideas contribute to cultural differences in social behavior.

5. In explaining our behavior we may ___dismiss___ factors that matter and ___inflate___ others that don't. We also poorly ___predict___ our own future behavior. Studies of perception and memory show that we are more aware of the ___results___ of our thinking that we are of the thinking ___process___.

6. We seem to have a ___dual___ attitude system, that is, an automatic ___implicit___ attitude and a differing consciously controlled, ___explicit___ attitude. People's errors in self-understanding place limits on the scientific usefulness of their ___self-reports___. Although personal testimonies are powerfully ___persuasive___, they may also convey unwitting error.

SELF-ESTEEM

7. Our self-esteem is our overall ___self-evaluation___. High self-esteem is generally more ___beneficial___ than low. However, after criticism, people with big egos are often ___aggressive___. Unlike a fragile self-esteem, a ___secure___ self-esteem—one rooted in internal rather than external sources—is conducive to long-term well-being.

PERCEIVED SELF-CONTROL

8. Bandura formulated the concept of ___self-efficacy___, that is, the sense that one is competent and effective. This sense leads us to set challenging ___goals___. It also predicts worker ___productivity___. Studies on locus of ___control___ and learned ___helplessness___ also indicate that feelings of self-determination facilitate achievement and coping.

SELF-SERVING BIAS

9. When perceiving ourselves we are prone to a potent error: ___self-serving___ bias. There is a tendency to blame the ___situation___ for our failures and to

accept _credit_ for our successes. The error is also evident in our tendency to see ourselves as generally _better_ than the _average_ person.

10. We demonstrate an unrealistic _optimism_ about future life events. We tend to _overestimate_ the commonality of our opinions and _underestimate_ the commonality of our abilities.

11. Self-serving perceptions arise partly from a motive to maintain and enhance _self-esteem_, a motive that protects people from _depression_ but that can also contribute to misjudgment and group _pride_, first among the seven deadly sins.

SELF-PRESENTATION

12. People sometimes present a different _self_ than they feel. The clearest example is false _modesty_. Sometimes people will even self-_handicap_ with self-defeating behaviors that protect self-esteem by providing excuses for _failure_.

13. _Self-presentation_ refers to our wanting to present a desired image both to other people and to _ourselves_. Those who score high on a scale of _self-monitoring_ tendency adjust their behavior to create the desired impression. The tendency to self-present modesty and restrained optimism is particularly great in cultures that value _self-restraint_.

MATCHING TERMS

Write the letter of the term on the right before the appropriate number on the left.

_c._   1.   Answer to the question, "Who am I?"
Self-concept

            a.   defensive pessimism

_e._   2.   The tendency to overestimate the emotional impact of future events.
Impact Bias

            b.   self-esteem

            c.   self-concept

_f._   3.   Beliefs about self that organize and guide the processing of self-relevant information.
Self-schema

            d.   self-serving bias

_h._   4.   The tendency to overestimate the commonality of one's undesirable behaviors.
false consensus effect

            e.   impact bias

            f.   self-schema

_n._   5.   The tendency to remember well information related to oneself.
self-reference effect

            g.   social identity

_l._   6.   Protecting one's self-image with behaviors that create a handy excuse for failure.
self handicapping

            h.   false consensus effect

_a._   7.   The adaptive value of anticipating problems and thereby avoiding unrealistic optimism.
defensive pessimism

            i.   illusion of transparency

_k._   8.   The belief that others are paying more attention to us than they really are.
Spotlight effect

            j.   self-monitoring

_d._   9.   May be a by-product of how we process information or a result of a self-esteem motivation.
Self-serving bias

            k.   spotlight effect

_j._   10.   Being attuned to the way one presents oneself in social situations and adjusting one's performance.
self-monitoring

            l.   self-handicapping

_m._   11.   The tendency to underestimate the commonality of one's abilities.
false uniqueness effect

            m.   false uniqueness effect

_g._   12.   The "we" aspect of our self-concept.
Social identity

            n.   self-reference effect

_i._   13.   The misperception that our concealed emotions can be easily read by others.
illusion of transparency

_b._   14.   A person's overall self-evaluation or sense of self-worth.
self-esteem

TRUE-FALSE REVIEW

Circle T if the statement is true and F if it is false.

T F 1. The self-reference effect illustrates how our sense of self is at the center of our worlds.

T F 2. People who took a pill that they thought would produce physical arousal tolerated much more shock than did people not given a pill.

T F 3. People are clearly aware of the factors that influence their daily moods.

T F 4. People are much better at predicting their own future behavior than that of others.

T F 5. Studies of perception and memory show that we are more aware of the <u>results</u> of our thinking than of its <u>process</u>.

T F 6. People's expressed attitudes are more likely to predict their behavior if people are first asked to analyze their feelings before indicating their attitudes.

T F 7. Suffering a paralyzing accident affects long-term happiness less than most people suppose.

T F 8. Our "possible selves" include images of the self we fear becoming as well as images of the self we dream of becoming.

T F 9. Japanese are more likely than Americans to complete the statement "I am" by stating their personal traits or personal goals.

T F 10. When we are feeling securely good about ourselves, we are more likely to berate people who don't like us.

T F 11. On nearly any dimension that is both subjective and socially desirable most people see themselves as better than average.

T F 12. No topic in psychology is today more researched than the self.

T F 13. In comparison to Americans, East Asians think more holistically—perceiving and thinking about objects and people in relationships to one another and to their environment.

T F 14. Compared to nondepressed people, depressed people make more accurate self-appraisals.

T F 15. The brain's right hemisphere plays an important role in self-recognition.

T (F) 16. Self-handicapping is typically motivated by feelings of inferiority.

(T) F 17. We can sometimes better predict people's behavior by asking them to predict others' actions rather than their own.

T (F) 18. The "spotlight effect" demonstrates how collectivists often suffer from low self-esteem.

(T) F 19. The more upset people are after a failure, the more likely they are to offer self-protective excuses.

(T) F 20. We more readily acknowledge our distant past failings than current ones.

T (F) 21. Self-serving bias seems to be restricted to people who live in North America and Europe.

T (F) 22. People with a strong sense of internal control believe that their destiny is controlled by other people.

T (F) 23. Martin Seligman maintains that schizophrenia is the result of learned helplessness.

(T) F 24. People with a strong sense of self-efficacy are less anxious and achieve more than do people who lack a sense of their own competence and effectiveness.

T (F) 25. When we give a speech, our nervousness is more apparent to our audience than we think it is.

MULTIPLE-CHOICE PRACTICE TEST

Circle the letter of the correct answer.

1. Our perceiving ourselves as athletic, overweight, smart, or shy constitutes our

   a. egocentric beliefs.
   b. interdependent self.
   (c) self-schemas.
   d. self-references.

2. According to Hazel Markus and her colleagues, our "possible selves"

   (a) include our vision of the self we dream of becoming and the self we fear becoming.
   b. include only our vision of the self we hope we will become.
   c. are the specific self-schemas that determine our self-esteem.
   d. are the ideal images that close friends and relatives have of us.

3. The tendency to process efficiently and remember well information related to oneself is called the _Self-reference_ effect.

    a. self-aggrandizing   c. self-processing
    b. self-schematizing   (d.) self-reference

4. Self-esteem refers to

    a. the sum total of our possible selves
    (b.) our overall self-evaluation
    c. the sum total of all our thoughts about ourselves
    d. our most central self-schemas

5. When people are asked whether they would comply with demands to deliver cruel shocks or would be hesitant to help a victim if several other people were present,

    (a.) they overwhelmingly deny their vulnerability to such influences.
    b. they admit they might be influenced but in their actual behavior are not.
    c. males deny they would be influenced, but females admit they would.
    d. they accurately predict their future behavior on such significant matters.

6. Research has indicated that when people are asked to record their daily mood and the factors that might influence it,

    (a.) there is little relationship between their perception of how important a factor was and how well the factor predicted their moods.
    b. females have better insight into what affects their moods than do males.
    c. people have much better insight into what influences their own moods than what influences the mood of a friend.
    d. adults have better insight into what affects their moods than do children.

7. Timothy Wilson suggests that the mental processes that _____ our social behavior are distinct from the mental processes through which we _____ our behavior.

    (a.) control; explain   c. produce; control
    b. evaluate; inhibit   d. form; change

8. In nine experiments, Timothy Wilson and his colleagues found that people's expressed attitudes predicted their later behavior reasonably well <u>unless</u>

    a. their attitudes were inconsistent with social norms.
    b. the experimenter had them under surveillance.
    (c.) they were asked to rationally analyze their feelings before indicating their attitudes.
    d. they had little opportunity to reflect on their feelings before indicating their attitudes.

9. According to the text, research on self-knowledge suggests that

    a. people tend to underestimate their own abilities
    b. people who have an interdependent self show less self-insight than those with an independent self
    c. people are highly accurate in predicting their own future behavior
    (d.) people's self-reports are often untrustworthy

10. In comparison to people in Western cultures, people in Asian cultures are more likely to demonstrate

    a. learned helplessness   c. self-serving bias
    b. self-handicapping   (d.) an interdependent self

11. What motto best represents societies that nurture an independent self?

    a. "No one is an island"
    b. "Birds of a feather flock together"
    (c.) "To thine own self be true"
    d. "One who hesitates is lost"

12. An internal locus of control is to _____ as unrealistic optimism is to _____.

    a. self-presentation; self-serving bias
    b. self-serving bias; fundamental attribution error
    (c.) self-efficacy; self-serving bias
    d. self-handicapping; self-efficacy

13. Bandura is to _____ as Rotter is to _____.

    a. learned helplessness; self-serving bias
    b. interdependent self; independent self
    (c.) self-efficacy; locus of control
    d. self-serving bias; fundamental attribution error

14. People who believe themselves internally controlled are more likely to

    a. take unnecessary risks
    b. engage in self-handicapping
    c. be tolerant of racial differences
    (d.) do well in school

15. Dogs who learn a sense of helplessness by being taught they cannot escape shocks

    a. tend to band together and as a group demonstrate collective efficacy
    b. tend to become highly aggressive in other situations
    c. more readily take the initiative to escape punishment when that becomes possible
    d. later fail to take the initiative in another situation when they can escape punishment

16. The fact that students tend to have a higher academic self-concept if they attend a school with few exceptionally capable students is best explained in terms of

    a. locus of control
    b. self-handicapping

    c. social comparison
    d. self-monitoring

17. Research findings challenge the notion that

    a. most people suffer from unrealistically low self-esteem
    b. we tend to blame others for their own misfortune
    c. we strive to protect and enhance our self-esteem
    d. true humility consists of self-forgetfulness

18. Charles H. Cooley's concept of the "looking-glass self" recognizes that our self-concept is shaped by

    a. the roles we play
    b. social comparison
    c. success and failure experiences
    d. other people's judgments

19. College students perceive themselves as far more likely than their classmates to _____ and as far less likely to _____

    a. draw a good salary; develop a drinking problem
    b. obtain a divorce; own a home
    c. travel to Europe; be happy in their work
    d. become a mental patient; have close friendships

20. We tend to _____ the commonality of our unsuccessful behaviors and _____ the commonality of our successful behaviors.

    a. overestimate; underestimate
    b. underestimate; overestimate

    c. underestimate; underestimate
    d. overestimate; overestimate

25

21. Gang leaders, extreme ethnocentrists, and terrorists tend to have _____ self-esteem.

   a. much lower than average
   b. somewhat lower than average
   c. average
   d. higher than average

22. The fact that we may have a habitual, automatic dislike of someone for whom we consciously verbalize respect illustrates

   a. our psychological immune system
   b. the illusion of transparency
   c. the conflict between our independent and interdependent selves
   d. our dual attitude system

23. Abraham Tesser has argued that a "_____" motive is important in helping us understand friction among brothers and sisters who share similar abilities.

   a. cognitive dissonance
   b. self-esteem maintenance
   c. self-forgetfulness
   d. social approval maintenance

24. Our ability to accommodate to major negative events (e.g. exam failures, romantic breakups) more readily that we would expect demonstrates the human tendency to

   a. immune neglect
   b. the illusion of control
   c. learned helplessness
   d. self-serving attribution

25. According to "terror management theory," positive self-esteem protects us from feeling anxiety over

   a. social rejection
   b. our own death
   c. public speaking
   d. failing to achieve an important goal

26. Those who do not exhibit self-serving bias may tend toward

   a. better than average mental health
   b. schizophrenia
   c. above average intelligence
   d. depression

27. Self-presentation, self-handicapping, and self-monitoring all reflect human efforts at

   a. self-efficacy
   b. self-understanding
   c. collective efficacy
   d. impression management

28. In contrast to those with an independent self-concept, those with an interdependent self-concept are most likely to disapprove of

   a. nationalism
   b. risk-taking
   c. conformity
   d. egotism

29. The self-handicapping strategy enables us to

    a. accept greater responsibility for our failures
    b. avoid the fundamental attribution error
    c. take greater credit for our successes
    d. circumvent the ill effects of the Peter Principle

30. Students are more likely to rate themselves as superior in _____ than in _____.

    a. moral goodness; intelligence
    b. being punctual; being disciplined
    c. creativity; honesty
    d. contributing money to the poor; caring for the poor

31. People are more modest when

    a. experts will be scrutinizing their self-evaluations
    b. they have a strong sense of self-efficacy
    c. they present themselves to others they regard as inferior
    d. they present themselves to members of their own family

32. Being attuned to the way one presents oneself in social situations and adjusting one's performance to create the desired impression is called

    a. self-handicapping   c. egocentric role-playing
    b. self-monitoring   d. manipulative social adjustment

33. In completing the statement, "I am…" Michelle responds by stating that she is the youngest in her family, belongs to a sorority, and is a member of the community orchestra. Michelle's statements most clearly reflect

    a. her possible selves   c. a self-serving bias
    b. an interdependent self   d. a strong self-monitoring tendency

34. Because she gets poor grades no matter how hard she studies, Milly has decided not to study at all. Milly's behavior most clearly demonstrates

    a. self-serving bias   c. learned helplessness
    b. unrealistic optimism   d. a self-monitoring tendency

35. Individualism is to _____ as collectivism is to _____.

    a. North American cultures; western European cultures
    b. industrialized Western cultures; Asian cultures
    c. third world cultures; Asian cultures
    d. Mexico; Canada

36. Betsy never plans ahead because she believes that the way things turn out is merely a matter of chance. Betsy's thinking most clearly illustrates

    a. the false uniqueness bias   c. self-handicapping
    b. an external locus of control   d. self-efficacy

37. Rahad was convinced that his classmates could detect his extreme anxiety when giving his oral book report. In fact, they all thought he was relaxed and confident. Rahad's misperception illustrates

    a. the self-reference effect   c. the illusion of transparency
    b. terror management   d. self-efficacy

38. Although Jeff frequently exceeds the speed limit by at least 10 miles per hour, he justifies his behavior by erroneously thinking that most other drivers do the same. His mistaken belief best illustrates

    a. learned helplessness   c. self-monitoring
    b. false consensus   d. an interdependent self

39. Those who evade paying income tax but who give generously to charity will probably _____ the number of others who evade taxes and _____ the number of others who give generously to charity.

    a. overestimate; overestimate   c. overestimate; underestimate
    b. underestimate; overestimate   d. underestimate; underestimate

40. Tomorrow morning Harry Smith has an interview that will determine whether he will be accepted into medical school. Rather than getting a good night's sleep, he is going to an all-night party with his friends. From the material presented in the text, which of the following may best describe Harry's behavior?

    a. Harry unconsciously hopes he is not accepted into medical school
    b. Harry is making the fundamental attribution error
    c. Harry is engaging in self-handicapping
    d. Harry shares with his friends a sense of collective efficacy

SHORT ESSAY QUESTIONS

Answer the following questions in the space provided.

1. Briefly explain what is meant by "self-schemas" and "possible selves."

   To guide our processing of self relevant information, and the images of what we dream or dread becoming that make up our possible selves.

   These are 2 elements of self concept.

2. Identify three factors that shape the development of one's self-concept.

   1) Social self: My roles as a student, family member, friend.

   2.) Self-esteem - My sense of self-worth

   3.) Self-knowledge - How can I explain & predict myself.

3. Discuss research findings regarding the accuracy of our self-knowledge.

   You can misread your own mind. Students endured a series of electric shocks. Some students took a fake pill said to increase heart palpitations, breathing troubles, etc. People that took the fake pill experienced 4 times as much shock as the ones that took the pill.

   People recorded their moods and rated different factors only to find out their was little relationships of how just a factor predicted their mood & how well it did.

4. Describe research findings on self-esteem.

   Students were given sets of three words like car, swimming, cue. They challenged them to think of a word that linked the three words. High self-esteem people were more likely to report having "integrative ability." If told it was important as opposed to being told it was useless.

5. What is self-efficacy? Briefly describe the results of research on this concept.

Self-efficacy - How competent we feel on a task on a task.

Older adults were shown words that evoked either a negative or positive stereotype of aging. Some were shown negative ones like decline, forgets, etc. Some shown positive ones. Seeing the positive words heightened better memory performance. Viewing the negative words had an opposite effect.

6. What is self-serving bias? Describe two lines of research that demonstrate the presence of the error.

Self-serving bias is the tendency to perceive oneself favorably.

In games athletes credit themselves when winning victories. When losing they blame it on bad calls, injuries, etc.

Drivers in accidents: "A pedestrian hit me and went under my car."

7. Explain how attempts at impression management may lead to false modesty and self-handicapping.

We are unaware of the impression we create and the way we act while trying to impress someone new that we become less modest. Unconsciously act different than we would with our friends.

30

Chapter Review

1. spotlight
   transparency

2. self
   reference
   schemas
   possible

3. roles
   comparisons
   judgments
   culture

4. individualism
   independent
   collectivism
   interdependent

5. dismiss
   inflate
   predict
   results
   process

6. dual
   implicit
   explicit
   self-reports
   persuasive

7. self-evaluation
   beneficial
   aggressive
   secure

8. self-efficacy
   goals
   productivity
   control
   helplessness

9. self-serving
   situation
   credit
   better
   average

10. optimism
    overestimate
    underestimate

11. self-esteem
    depression
    pride

12. self
    modesty
    handicap
    failure

13. Self-presentation
    ourselves
    self-monitoring
    self-restraint

Matching Terms

1.	c	8.	k
2.	e	9.	d
3.	f	10.	j
4.	h	11.	m
5.	n	12.	g
6.	l	13.	i
7.	a	14.	b

True-False Review

1.	T	14.	T
2.	T	15.	T
3.	F	16.	F
4.	F	17.	T
5.	T	18.	F
6.	F	19.	T
7.	T	20.	T
8.	T	21.	F
9.	F	22.	F
10.	F	23.	F
11.	T	24.	T
12.	T	25.	F
13.	T		

Multiple-Choice Practice Test

1. c		21. d
2. a		22. d
3. d		23. b
4. b		24. a
5. a		25. b
6. a		26. d
7. a		27. d
8. c		28. d
9. d		29. c
10. d		30. a
11. c		31. a
12. c		32. b
13. c		33. b
14. d		34. c
15. d		35. b
16. c		36. b
17. a		37. c
18. d		38. b
19. a		39. c
20. a		40. c

CHAPTER 3

SOCIAL BELIEFS AND JUDGMENTS

CHAPTER OBJECTIVES

After completing your study of this chapter you should be able to:

1. Show how our preconceptions control our interpretations and memories.

2. Illustrate and explain the overconfidence phenomenon.

3. Describe the representativeness and availability heuristics.

4. Illustrate the illusions of correlation and personal control.

5. Describe how our moods affect our judgments.

6. Identify the assumptions, questions, and general findings of attribution theory.

7. Define the fundamental attribution error, and explain why it occurs.

8. Describe how our erroneous beliefs may generate their own reality.

CHAPTER REVIEW

Supply the words necessary to complete each of the following statements.
PERCEIVING OUR SOCIAL WORLD

1. Certain experiments show that people's preconceived notions bias the way they perceive and _interpret_ information they are given. _Priming_ is the activating of certain associations in memory. The effect of prior beliefs on social perception is so great that even _contradictory_ evidence may be seen as supporting one's beliefs.

2. Studies indicate that a falsehood is difficult to demolish if people have invented an _explanation_ for it. The belief perseverance phenomenon can be reduced by having people explain the _opposite_ . Research also indicates that we easily (though unconsciously) revise our _memories_ . We _reconstruct_ our past attitudes and past behavior.

JUDGING OUR SOCIAL WORLD

3. Our thinking is partly controlled and partly _automatic_ . Our cognitive efficiency comes at the cost of occasional _error_ . For example, people tend to be more _confident_ than correct.

4. The overconfidence phenomenon seems partly due to the fact that people are more likely to search for information that _confirms_ their beliefs than for information that does not. Overconfidence can be reduced by giving people prompt _feedback_ on the accuracy of their judgments and by getting them to think of one good reason why their judgments might be _wrong_ .

5. We use mental shortcuts called _heuristics_ to form impressions, make judgments, and invent explanations. To judge something by intuitively comparing it to our mental representation of a category is to use the _representativeness_ heuristic.

6. People are _below_ to deduce particular instances from a general truth but are _quick_ to infer general truth from a vivid instance. If examples are readily _available_ in our memory, we presume that the event is commonplace.

7. People also tend to see _correlation_ where none exists. They readily perceive random events as _confirming_ their beliefs.

8. Our tendency to perceive random events as though they were related feeds the illusion that chance events are subject to our _influence_ . Ellen Langer demonstrated the illusion with experiments on _gambling_ . The illusion of control may arise as a result of the statistical phenomenon of _regression_ toward the _average person_ .

9. Our _mood_ color how we recall and interpret our world. In a _bad_ mood, we have more depressing thoughts.

EXPLAINING OUR SOCIAL WORLD

10. _attribution_ theory analyzes how we explain people's behavior. It suggests we explain others' behavior either in terms of _internal_ or _external_ causes.

11. Edward Jones and Keith Davis noted that we often infer that people's dispositions _correspond_ to their actions. Harold Kelley described how we use

36

information about _consistency_, distinctiveness, and _consensus_ in explaining behavior. Kelley also found that people often _discount_ a contributing cause of behavior if other plausible causes are already known.

12. The "_fundamental_ attribution error" refers to the tendency for observers to underestimate _situational_ influences and to overestimate _dispositional_ influences upon others' behavior.

13. Even when people know they are _causing_ someone else's behavior, they still underestimate _external_ influences.

14. We commit this error when explaining _others_ behavior. We often explain our own behavior in terms of the _situation_ while attributing others' behavior to their _dispositions_.

15. Why do we make this attributional error? Attribution theorists point out that we have a different _perspective_ when observing than when acting. When we watch another person act, the _person_ occupies the center of our attention. When we act, the _environment_ commands our attention. Perspectives can change with _time_ and circumstances. If people are made _self-conscious_, they attribute more responsibility to themselves.

16. Other explanations have been offered for the fundamental attribution error. For example, our whole Western worldview inclines us to assume that _people_, not _situations_, cause events.

17. The fundamental attribution error is fundamental because it colors our _explanations_ in basic and important ways. For example, people's attributions predict their _attitudes_ toward the poor and unemployed.

EXPECTATIONS OF OUR SOCIAL WORLD

18. Studies of _experimenter_ bias and teacher expectations illustrate the _self-fulfilling_ prophecy: a belief that leads to its own fulfillment.

CONCLUSIONS

19. A balanced social psychology appreciates both the powers and the _perils_ of social thinking.

MATCHING TERMS

Write the letter of the term on the right before the appropriate number on the left.

_____   1. Throwing dice softly for low numbers and   a. priming
                and hard for high numbers.
                                                                   b. misinformation effect
_____   2. Clinging to beliefs in spite of contradictory
                evidence.   c. illusion of control

_____   3. Activating particular associations in   d. regression toward the
                memory.   average

_____   4. Searching for information that confirms one's   e. counterfactual thinking
                expectations.
                                                                   f. availability heuristic
_____   5. Shows how memory is constructive.
                                                                   g. overconfidence
_____   6. A false belief that leads to its own   phenomenon
                fulfillment.
                                                                   h. self-fulfilling prophecy
_____   7. It analyzes how we make judgments about
                people.   i. belief perseverance

_____   8. Perceiving order in random events.   j. illusory correlation

_____   9. High scorers on one exam obtain lower scores   k. attribution theory
                on the next exam.
                                                                   l. fundamental attribution
_____   10. Imagining what might have happened but   error
                didn't.
                                                                   m. representativeness
_____   11. Presuming, despite contrary odds, that someone   heuristic
                belongs to a particular group if resembling a
                typical member.   n. confirmation bias

_____   12. The tendency to overestimate the
                the accuracy of one's beliefs.

_____   13. The tendency for observers to underestimate
                situational influences and overestimate
                dispositional influences.

_____   14. Judging the likelihood of events in terms of how
                quickly they come to mind.

Circle T if the statement is true and F if it is false.

T F   1. Attribution theorists are primarily concerned with how we are influenced by others, particularly by groups.

T F   2. Fritz Heider concluded that people tend to attribute someone's behavior either to stable or to unstable factors.

T F   3. According to the text, we often form judgments of one another in a reasonable manner.

T F   4. Discounting of situational effects in judging another's behavior is called the *fundamental attribution error*.

T F   5. Harold Kelley suggests that we use information about "correspondence" in judging the causes of another's behavior.

T F   6. We often explain our own behavior in terms of the situation while holding others responsible for their behavior.

T F   7. Counterfactual thinking underlies our feeling of both good and bad luck.

T F   8. Memory is like a storage chest into which we deposit material. Occasionally something gets lost from the chest, and then we say we have forgotten.

T F   9. Memories are often reconstructions of the past.

T F 10. The Kulechov effect refers to the fact that collectivists are less vulnerable to the fundamental attribution error.

T F 11. About 30 percent of the time, the correct answers lay outside the range about which people feel 98 percent confident.

T F 12. People tend to seek out confirming rather than disconfirming evidence for their beliefs.

T F 13. Providing people with prompt feedback on the accuracy of their judgments reduces the overconfidence phenomenon.

T F 14. Research indicates that, with the passage of time, we are more likely to explain election outcomes in terms of situational factors than in terms of candidates' traits and positions.

T F 15. "Regression toward the average" refers to our tendency to be conformist.

T F 16. Hindsight bias explains why people are more afraid of flying than driving.

T F 17. The availability heuristic provides an explanation for the self-fulfilling prophecy.

T F 18. People are slow to deduce particular instances from a general truth but are quick to infer general truth from a vivid instance.

T F 19. People who chose a lottery number for themselves demanded four times as much money for the sale of their lottery ticket than people whose number was assigned by the experimenter.

T F 20. "Regression toward the average" may help to explain why the illusion of control arises.

T F 21. The results of experimenter bias demonstrate the tendency of one's expectations to evoke behavior that confirms the expectations.

T F 22. Cases of blindsight illustrate how people may know more than they know they know.

T F 23. Research indicates that children but not adults construct false memories.

T F 24. Simple, efficient thinking strategies that help us simplify and cope with reality are known as *schemata*.

T F 25. Most published experiments have confirmed that teachers' expectations significantly influence their students' performance.

MULTIPLE-CHOICE PRACTICE TEST

Circle the letter of the correct answer.

1. People who were shown the random mix of results from a 50-day cloud-seeding experiment made judgments that showed

   a. an illusory correlation
   b. the base-rate fallacy
   c. the misinformation effect
   d. counterfactual thinking

2. Women's friendliness is especially likely to be misread as a sexual come-on by men who

   a. have no sisters
   b. are in positions of power
   c. have low self-esteem
   d. have liberal political attitudes

3. In Olympic competition, _____ medalists exhibit more joy than _____ medalists.

   a. bronze; silver
   b. silver; bronze
   c. bronze; gold
   d. silver; gold

4. In a series of experiments, Elizabeth Loftus has had people witness an effect, receive misleading information about it, and then take a memory test. The repeated finding is

   a. the misinformation effect
   b. counterfactual thinking
   c. confirmation bias
   d. information integration

5. The more closely we examine our theories and explain how they might be true,

   a. the more uncertain we become of them
   b. the more closed we become to discrediting information
   c. the more open we are likely to become to discrediting information
   d. the more complex our theories are likely to become

6. The tendency of people to cling to their ideas even in the face of contrary evidence is called the

   a. belief perseverance phenomenon
   b. availability heuristic
   c. belief assimilation phenomenon
   d. denial paradox

7. The Kulechov effect, in which people perceive different emotions in an actor's face, illustrates

   a. the availability heuristic
   b. memory construction
   c. our use of useless information
   d. how preconceptions control our interpretations

8. The tendency of people to cling to their ideas even in the face of contrary evidence can be reduced by having them

   a. study the hindsight bias
   b. study the evidence more carefully
   c. participate in a debate
   d. explain why the opposite idea might be true

9. In recalling a scene from our past experience we often see ourselves in the scene. This illustrates how

   a. memory is a reconstruction of the past
   b. memory always involves mental imagery
   c. personal memories are often precise copies of the past
   d. memory is heuristic

10. Cases of blindsight and studies of subliminal stimulation demonstrate how

   a. thinking is partly automatic
   b. memory is reconstructive
   c. preconceptions shape interpretations
   d. beliefs can be self-fulfilling

11. Rob Holland and his colleagues reported that Dutch students who were exposed to the scent of an all-purpose cleaner were quicker to identify cleaning-related words. This finding provides a good example of the

   a. effects of the representativeness heuristic
   b. complex dynamics of belief perseverance
   c. impact of priming
   d. power of self-fulfilling prophecy

12. Giving people immediate feedback on the accuracy of their judgments

   a. reduces the overconfidence bias
   b. shows no effect on the overconfidence bias
   c. reduces overconfidence bias in children but not in adults
   d. undermines their self-confidence and leads them to make worse errors in judgment

13. Research indicates that participants in self-improvement programs show _____ improvement on average and claim they received _____ improvement.

   a. considerable; modest   c. modest; modest
   b. modest; considerable   d. considerable; considerable

14. The incorrect belief that the letter "k" appears more often as the first letter of a word than as the third letter can be understood in terms of

   a. the availability heuristic   c. regression toward the average
   b. hindsight bias   d. the illusion of control

15. After a 1990 football game between Alabama and Auburn, victorious Alabama fans viewed _____ than did the losing Auburn fans.

    a. war as more likely and advantageous to the United States
    b. war as less likely and potentially devastating
    c. a college degree as less necessary and enriching
    d. a college degree as more valuable and enriching

16. Tversky and Kahneman have identified _____ as a possible cause of the illusion of control.

    a. schemata   c. self-fulfilling prophecy
    b. base-rate fallacy   d. regression toward the average

17. The theory of how we explain others' behavior is known as

    a. impression theory
    b. inferential analysis theory
    c. cognitive dissonance theory
    d. attribution theory

18. According to the theory of correspondent inferences,

    a. we tend to infer that people's intentions and dispositions correspond to their actions
    b. we tend to infer that people's intentions and dispositions correspond to our own intentions and dispositions
    c. we tend to infer that people share the same underlying motives and values
    d. those who have similar values tend to make the same attributions about others

19. For a school debate, Sally has been asked to argue in favor of capital punishment. Research on the fundamental attribution error suggests that observers of Sally's speech will conclude that her arguments

    a. reflect her true attitude on the topic
    b. reflect a tendency to present herself favorably
    c. are weak because she was assigned to present a particular position on the topic
    d. will lead her to experience cognitive dissonance

20. The tendency for observers to underestimate the impact of the situation and overestimate the impact of inner dispositions upon another's behavior is called

    a. the self-serving bias   c. the fundamental attribution error
    b. the false consensus bias   d. cognitive conceit

21. Hearing scary ghost stories may cause us to misinterpret the sound of a delivery person as a burglar. This illustrates

    a. the fundamental attribution error   c. self-fulfilling prophecy
    b. counterfactual thinking   d. the process of priming

22. When subjects were informed that debaters had been told to take a pro-Castro or an anti-Castro position in their speeches, they judged

    a. the debaters to be insincere and hypocritical
    b. that the stated positions were coerced and did not reflect the debaters' attitudes
    c. that the stated positions still reflected the debaters' true attitudes
    d. the debaters to be cooperative but uninformed

23. People from collectivist cultures are more likely than Americans to

    a. offer situational explanations for someone's actions
    b. offer dispositional explanations for someone's actions
    c. engage in self-handicapping
    d. offer self-serving explanations for their own behavior

24. There is a tendency to attribute the causes of _____ behavior to the situation and to attribute the causes of _____ behavior to traits.

    a. our own; others'   c. children's; adults'
    b. others'; our own   d. males'; females'

25. Our tendency to attribute others' behavior to their personal characteristics is reduced when we

    a. view a videotape of the behavior recorded from their perspective
    b. make judgments about criminal behavior
    c. are high in self-efficacy
    d. make judgments about academic performance

26. According to Harold Kelley's theory of attributions, the three factors that influence whether we attribute someone's behavior to internal or external causes are

    a. distinctiveness, consensus, relevance
    b. distinctiveness, consensus, consistency
    c. relevance, consistency, consensus
    d. distinctiveness, consistency, relevance

27. According to the text, the fundamental attribution error may lead us to

    a. overestimate the brilliance of our teachers
    b. fail to hold people responsible for their misconduct
    c. be lenient with convicted criminals
    d. underestimate our own compassion

28. Studies of experimenter bias and teacher expectations have revealed the presence of

    a. hindsight bias   c. self-fulfilling prophecy
    b. illusory correlation   d. a fundamental attribution error

29. Nisbett and Ross believe that education could reduce our vulnerability to errors in social thinking and should include

    a. teaching useful slogans such as "It's an empirical question"
    b. teaching that is illustrated with vivid anecdotes and examples
    c. statistics courses that are geared to everyday problems of logic
    d. all of these

30. The textbook states that a large drop in prices on the stock market sometimes illustrates

    a. the representativeness heuristic   c. the overconfidence phenomenon
    b. the availability heuristic   d. self-fulfilling prophecy

31. You notice that Mary has missed class, and you commit the fundamental attribution error by thinking,

    a. Mary has been required to work overtime
    b. Mary is lazy
    c. Mary's friends stopped by her room unexpectedly
    d. Mary has the flu

32. As a result of making the fundamental attribution error you might be likely to favor

    a. increases in unemployment benefits
    b. increases in international aid to poor countries
    c. more severe penalties for criminal offenses
    d. victim compensation laws

33. Although Fred was certain he answered at least 50 items correctly on his history test, he actually was right on only 40 items. Fred's misjudgment illustrates

    a. the self-fulfilling prophecy   c. the overconfidence phenomenon
    b. the hindsight bias   d. regression toward the average

34. Linda is 31, single, and outspoken. As a college student she was deeply concerned with discrimination and other social issues. A tendency to conclude that it is more likely that Linda is a bank teller and active in the feminist movement than simply a bank teller illustrates the powerful influence of

   a. belief perseverance
   b. the availability heuristic
   c. regression toward the average
   d. the representativeness heuristic

35. Despite reading solid research evidence that cigarette smoking causes cancer, Philip continues to believe that smoking is harmless. Philip's thinking clearly reveals

   a. belief assimilation
   b. belief consolidation
   c. belief perseverance
   d. operation of the availability heuristic

36. Many people firmly believe in astrology's ability to predict the future. Assuming they are presented a history of an astrologer's past predictions, which in actuality show a random mix of success and failure, they are likely to

   a. believe the astrologer is successful
   b. question this astrologer's predictive ability but still believe in the validity of astrology
   c. become very defensive
   d. give up their belief in the validity of astrology

37. Bob, a baseball player, makes five hits whereas Joe, a member of the same team, makes none in a particular game. In the next game, both obtain one hit. What term used in the text explains Bob's fewer hits and Joe's increase?

   a. overconfidence bias
   b. priming
   c. regression to the average
   d. schemata

38. What psychological term might best be used to describe the rule "I before E except after C"?

   a. base-rate fallacy
   b. hindsight bias
   c. illusion of control
   d. heuristic

39. A person enters a casino and after inserting one silver dollar in a slot machine hits the jackpot. This person's tendency to continue putting money into the machine so that finally the amount lost exceeds the original winnings can perhaps best be explained in terms of

   a. self-fulfilling prophecy
   b. regression toward the average
   c. illusion of control
   d. hindsight bias

40. The people in a small town become convinced that the bank where they have their savings accounts is unsound. The next day, most of them demand their savings. By the end of the day, the bank is unable to pay off all those who want their deposits. This is an example of

    a. regression toward the average   c. the hindsight bias
    b. self-fulfilling prophecy   d. illusory correlation

SHORT ESSAY QUESTIONS

Answer the following questions in the space provided.

1. Describe what is meant by the term *memory construction*.

To reconstruct our distant past by using our current feelings and expectations to combine information fragments

2. Give one reason why we are overconfident.

Being ignorant of our ignorance. Recalling mistaken judgements as times when they were almost right

3. Distinguish between the availability heuristic and the representativeness heuristic.

4. Provide one example of illusory correlation and one example of the illusion of control.

An example of illusory correlation is thinking about a friend, that friend calls us then we notice such a coincidence. However, we don't notice thoughts about a friend without receiving a call from a friend we hadn't been thinking about.

An example of illusion of control - compared to people given an assigned lottery number, the one's who chose their own number demanded four times as much money when asked if they would sell their ticket.

5. Briefly describe the central concern of attribution theory. According to Fritz Heider, to what two kinds of causes do we attribute behavior?

Making casual explanations. Explaining other's behavior.
We attribute behavior by internal cause the (person's disposition) and external causes (something about the person's situation.)

6. What is the fundamental attribution error? Why does it occur?

The fundamental attribution error is for observers to underestimate situational influences and overestimate dispositional influences upon others behavior. We attribute their behavior so much to their inner traits and attitudes that we discount situational constraints, even when those are obvious.

7. Discuss the implications of self-fulfilling prophecy for the classroom.

ANSWER KEY

Chapter Review

1. interpret
   Priming
   contradictory

2. explanation
   opposite
   memories
   reconstruct

3. automatic
   error
   confident

4. confirms
   feedback
   wrong

5. heuristics
   representativeness

6. slow
   quick
   available

7. correlation
   confirming

8. influence
   gambling
   regression
   average

9. moods
   bad

10. Attribution
    internal
    external

11. correspond
    consistency
    consensus
    discount

12. fundamental
    situational
    dispositional

13. causing
    external

14. others'
    situation
    dispositions

15. perspective
    person
    environment
    time
    self-conscious

16. people
    situations

17. explanations
    attitudes

18. experimenter
    self-fulfilling

19. perils

Matching Terms

1. c	8. j
2. i	9. d
3. a	10. e
4. n	11. m
5. b	12. g
6. h,	13. l
7. k	14. f

True-False Review

1. F	14. T
2. F	15. F
3. T	16. F
4. T	17. F
5. F	18. T
6. T	19. T
7. T	20. T
8. F	21. T
9. T	22. T
10. T	23. F
11. T	24. F
12. T	25. F
13. T	

Multiple-Choice Practice Test

1.	a	21.	d
2.	b	22.	c
3.	a	23.	a
4.	a	24.	a
5.	b	25.	a
6.	a	26.	b
7.	d	27.	a
8.	d	28.	c
9.	a	29.	d
10.	a	30.	d
11.	c	31.	b
12.	a	32.	c
13.	b	33.	c
14.	a	34.	d
15.	b	35.	c
16.	d	36.	a
17.	d	37.	c
18.	a	38.	d
19.	a	39.	c
20.	c	40.	b

CHAPTER 4

BEHAVIOR AND ATTITUDES

After completing your study of this chapter you should be able to:

1. Identify the components of an attitude.

2. Describe research findings on the relationship between attitudes and behavior.

3. Identify the conditions under which attitudes predict behavior.

4. Provide evidence that behavior determines attitudes.

5. Give three explanations for why our actions affect our attitudes.

6. Describe how rewards influence attitudes.

CHAPTER REVIEW

Supply the words necessary to complete each of the following statements.

1. An attitude is a favorable or unfavorable _____ reaction toward something or someone, often rooted in one's _____, and exhibited in one's feelings and intended _____.

HOW WELL DO OUR ATTITUDES PREDICT OUR BEHAVIOR?

2. Allan Wicker's review of research findings led social psychologists to question whether _____ determine _____. Research also suggested that attempts to change _____ by changing attitudes often _____. As a result, the developing picture of what controls our behavior seemed to focus on _____ factors.

3. Social psychologists never get a direct reading on people's attitudes. Instead they measure _____ attitudes, which like other behaviors, are subject to _____ influences. The implicit _____ test is a subtle attitude measure that uses reaction times to measure how quickly people associate concepts.

4. Attitudes predict behavior when other _____ upon our behavior are minimal, when the attitude is specifically _____ to the observed behavior, and when the attitude is _____. Much of our behavior is _____ as we act out familiar scripts without reflecting on what we're doing. Making people _____ promotes consistency between words and deeds.

WHEN DOES OUR BEHAVIOR AFFECT OUR ATTITUDES?

5. An important lesson recent social psychology teaches is that we are likely not only to _____ ourselves into a way of acting but also to _____ ourselves into a way of thinking.

6. For example, the actions prescribed by a social _____ readily mold a person's attitudes. People come to believe what they _____, provided they are not bribed or coerced into doing so. Research on the _____ phenomenon indicates that performing a small act (for example, agreeing to do a small favor) later makes people more willing to do a larger one.

7. _____ acts corrode one's conscience, and oppressors frequently _____ their victims. Fortunately the principle works in the other direction as well. _____ action strengthens one's conscience.

8. More positive interracial behavior may lead to the reduction of racial _____. Brainwashing includes a gradual _____ of demands and active _____ in an attempt to change a person's loyalties.

WHY DOES OUR BEHAVIOR AFFECT OUR ATTITUDES?

9. _____ theory assumes that people express attitudes in line with their _____ to create a good impression.

10. Cognitive _____ theory states that people are motivated to justify their behavior after acting contrary to their attitudes or after making a difficult _____. The theory further proposes that the less _____ justification we have for an undesirable action the more we feel _____ for it and thus the more _____ is aroused and the more our attitudes change.

54

11. _____ theory assumes that when we are _____ of our attitudes we simply observe our _____ and its circumstances and infer what our attitudes must be. An important implication of this theory is the _____ effect: Rewarding people to do what they like doing anyway turns their pleasure into work.

12. _____ theory states that people who experience a self-image threat compensate by affirming another aspect of the self. Dissonance theory explains attitude _____ whereas self-perception theory explains attitude _____.

MATCHING TERMS

Write the letter of the term on the right before the appropriate number on the left.

_____	1. Participants showed a growing confusion between role-playing and self-identity.	a.	attitude
		b.	role
_____	2. Suggests that when people's self-concept is threatened, they may compensate by doing good deeds.	c.	self-affirmation theory
		d.	low-ball technique
_____	3. A consequence of bribing people to do what they already like doing.	e.	cognitive dissonance
_____	4. Actions expected of those who occupy a particular social position.	f.	self-presentation theory
_____	5. Includes beliefs, feelings, and behavior tendencies.	g.	insufficient justification effect
_____	6. Reduction of dissonance by internally justifying one's behavior when external inducements do not fully justify it.	h.	self-perception theory
_____	7. Uses principle of active participation to shape thought.	i.	overjustification effect
_____	8. Uses reaction times to measure how quickly people associate concepts.	j.	brainwashing
_____	9. A technique for getting people to agree to do something.	k.	Stanford prison simulation
_____	10. Expressing oneself and behaving in ways designed to create a favorable impression or an impression that corresponds to one's ideals.	l.	implicit association test
_____	11. When we are unsure of our attitudes we infer them by examining our behavior.		
_____	12. Tension that results when two beliefs are inconsistent.		

TRUE-FALSE REVIEW

Circle T if the statement is true and F if it is false.

T F 1. An attitude is composed of beliefs, feelings, and inclinations to act.

T F 2. Allan Wicker reported that the expressed attitudes of a group of people predict about 90 percent of the variations in their behaviors.

T F 3. People's expressed religious attitudes show no relationship to the total quantity of their religious behaviors over a period of time.

T F 4. The implicit association test is a fake lie detector.

T F 5. Attitudes toward recycling predict participation in recyling.

T F 6. People's expressed attitudes predict their average behavior much better than their behavior in a specific situation.

T F 7. The text states that increasing public awareness about the brutalizing effects of television violence has dramatically changed what people choose to watch.

T F 8. Guards and prisoners in the Stanford prison simulation quickly absorbed the roles they played.

T F 9. Social psychologists sometimes measure facial muscle responses to assess people's attitude about a given statement.

T F 10. Experiments indicate that positive behavior toward someone fosters liking for that person.

T F 11. "Low-balling" is an example of the overjustification effect.

T F 12. The low-ball technique has proven to be ineffective because it assumes that attitudes determine behavior.

T F 13. Research indicates that if people have granted a small request they are more likely to refuse to grant a larger request made later.

T F 14. Severe threats tend to be more effective than mild threats in getting children to internalize a moral principle.

T F 15. Research on racial attitudes and behavior suggests that to change racial behavior one must first change racial attitudes.

T F 16. A gradual escalation of demands and active participation are both components of effective brainwashing.

T F 17. People with high and secure self-esteem engage in less self-justification.

T F 18. The "principle of aggregation" refers to the combined effects of several behaviors on a given attitude.

T F 19. Dissonance theory predicts that when there is external justification for performing an act, dissonance will be high.

T F 20. Self-perception theory assumes that we infer our own attitudes by looking at our behavior.

T F 21. Dissonance is likely to occur after making an important and difficult decision.

T F 22. The greater the reward promised for an activity, the more one will come to enjoy the activity.

T F 23. The principle that attitudes follow behavior is predictable from more than one theory.

T F 24. Research indicates that alcohol can provide a substitute way to reduce dissonance.

T F 25. Cognitive dissonance theory provides a better explanation for the overjustification effect than does self-perception theory.

MULTIPLE-CHOICE PRACTICE TEST

Circle the correct letter.

1. The "ABC's of attitudes" refers to

   a. aptitudes, brainwashing, and cognition
   b. attraction, behavior, and compliance
   c. affect, behavior, and cognition
   d. affect, bogus pipeline, and cognitive dissonance

2. In 1971, social psychologist Allan Wicker said, "It may be desirable to abandon the attitude concept." Wicker made this statement because

    a. no one could provide an adequate measure of attitudes
    b. attitudes did not seem to have much effect on behavior
    c. social psychologists could not agree on a definition of an attitude
    d. the study of attitudes had obscured the study of other influences on behavior

3. Which of the following is a technique for measuring attitudes?

    a. self-monitoring pipeline   c. low-ball technique
    b. foot-in-the-door phenomenon   d. implicit association test

4. Daniel Batson and his colleagues found that when research participants could assign themselves or someone else to an appealing versus a dull task, most

    a. felt that assigning themselves to the appealing task was the moral thing to do
    b. assigned themselves to the appealing task
    c. asked someone else to make the assignment
    d. made the assignment on the basis of a coin flip

5. Based on recent social-psychological research, which of the following statements is true?

    a. Our attitudes and our behavior are unrelated
    b. Our attitudes determine our behavior, but our behavior does not determine our attitudes
    c. Our behavior determines our attitudes, but our attitudes do not determine our behavior
    d. Under certain circumstances attitudes do predict behavior

6. In their studies of moral hypocrisy, Daniel Batson and his colleagues found that _____ brought behavior in line with espoused moral attitudes.

    a. rewards
    b. mirrors
    c. forewarnings
    d. appeals to moral or altruistic norms

7. Research suggests that to change health habits through persuasion, we should alter people's attitudes toward

    a. specific health practices
    b. the general concept of "health fitness"
    c. health authorities
    d. the value of life itself

8. According to the text, our attitudes will predict our behavior if

    a. we are made aware of social norms
    b. the attitudes are unrelated to central values
    c. as we act, we are conscious of our attitudes
    d. we feel anxious or insecure

9. Rewards and praise that inform people of their achievements _____ intrinsic motivation. Rewards that seek to control people _____ intrinsic motivation.

    a. strengthen; strengthen   c. strengthen; weaken
    b. weaken; strengthen   d. weaken; weaken

10. Gary Wells and Richard Petty found that people were more likely to agree with a radio editorial if they _____ while listening to it.

    a. moved their heads up and down
    b. stuck out their tongues
    c. moved their heads left to right
    d. drank strong coffee and ate donuts

11. Researchers found that after complying with a request to display a 3-inch "Be a safe driver" sign, Californians were

    a. more likely to obey traffic laws
    b. more likely to break the speed limit
    c. less likely to comply later with a request to place a large, ugly "Drive Carefully" sign in their front yards
    d. more likely to comply later with a request to place a large, ugly "Drive Carefully" sign in their front yards

12. The tendency for oppressors to disparage their victims is given in the text as an example of

    a. how attitudes determine behavior
    b. how behavior determines attitudes
    c. the low-balling effect
    d. how role playing comes to shape one's self-identity

13. Which of the following is cited in the text as an example of how changing behavior can alter attitudes?

    a. civil rights legislation   c. traffic laws
    b. prohibition   d. capital punishment legislation

14. The text suggests that Americans' revised memories of why their government entered into the 2003 Iraq war fits the claims of _____ theory.

   a. cognitive dissonance
   b. self-presentation
   c. self-perception
   d. reinforcement

15. The theory that states that we adopt certain attitudes in order to justify our past actions is _____ theory.

   a. cognitive dissonance
   b. self-presentation
   c. self-perception
   d. psychological reactance

16. Research has indicated that racetrack bettors who have just placed their bets are

   a. more optimistic about their bet than those who are about to bet
   b. less confident about their bet than those who are about to bet
   c. less enthusiastic about the sport of horse racing than those who are about to bet
   d. more susceptible to persuasive attempts than those who are about to bet

17. Which of the following is not given in the text as an example of how behavior shapes attitudes?

   a. brainwashing of American POWs
   b. children's resistance to temptation
   c. the old German greeting of "Heil Hitler"
   d. the bogus-pipeline effect

18. The gradual escalation of demands and active participation were described as key elements in

   a. the overjustification effect
   b. brainwashing
   c. the underjustification effect
   d. the low-balling effect

19. Which of the following theories suggests that people express attitudes in line with how they acted in order to avoid looking foolishly inconsistent?

   a. cognitive dissonance theory
   b. self-perception theory
   c. self-presentation theory
   d. role-playing theory

20. According to the text, we are least likely to feel dissonance when we

   a. have made a difficult decision
   b. do not feel responsible for our behavior
   c. have harmed a friend
   d. have been paid a small sum of money for telling a lie

21. The author of cognitive dissonance theory was

   a. Wicker
   b. Bem
   c. Festinger
   d. Bandura

22. According to self-perception theory, behavior shapes attitudes

   a. only of self-monitoring people
   b. when behavior is inconsistent with attitudes
   c. when attitudes are weak and ambiguous
   d. only in the area of politics and religion

23. When severe and mild threats were used in an attempt to prevent children from engaging in a prohibited activity,

   a. only the severe threat was strong enough to deter the children from engaging in the prohibited activity
   b. both threats deterred the children, but children given the mild threat showed greater internalization of the rule
   c. both threats deterred the children, but children given the severe threat showed greater internalization of the rule
   d. neither threat was successful in getting the children to internalize the rule

24. College students experienced more empathy for a victim receiving electric shock when they were told

   a. something about the victim's life history
   b. that the victim would later be compensated for receiving the shock
   c. that the victim would later reverse roles with the person delivering the shock
   d. to imitate the victim's expression of pain

25. Both cognitive dissonance theory and self-perception theory provide an explanation for the

   a. hindsight bias
   b. insufficient justification effect
   c. overjustification effect
   d. self-monitoring tendency

26. According to self-perception theory, rewards do not diminish intrinsic interest if

   a. the rewards are unanticipated
   b. the rewards are large
   c. the rewards are small
   d. social approval accompanies any monetary reward

27. The theory that best explains the overjustification effect is

    a. cognitive dissonance theory
    b. self-presentation theory
    c. self-perception theory
    d. aggregation theory

28. Students who had been induced to write an essay favoring a big tuition increase reduced their dissonance by adjusting their attitudes unless

    a. after writing the essay they drank alcohol
    b. they were related to the administrators at the college
    c. they were college seniors
    d. they were self-monitoring persons

29. According to the text, which of the following is true of self-perception and cognitive dissonance theories?

    a. Self-perception theory has significantly more support than cognitive dissonance theory
    b. Cognitive dissonance theory has been proven correct, and self-perception theory is still being tested
    c. They are contradictory theories; therefore both cannot have validity
    d. Evidence exists to support both theories, suggesting wisdom in both

30. Self-perception theory is to _____ as dissonance theory is to _____.

    a. attitude formation; attitude change
    b. attitude change; attitude formation
    c. impression formation; self-monitoring
    d. self-monitoring; impression formation

31. According to Claude Steele, people are aroused by their dissonant behavior because it often

    a. leads to physical punishment
    b. challenges their sense of purpose or meaning in life
    c. threatens their sense of self-worth
    d. leads to social rejection

32. Which of the following is a component of Mary's attitude toward smoking?

    a. Mary believes smoking is harmful to one's health
    b. Mary dislikes the fact that people are permitted to smoke in vehicles of public transportation
    c. Mary is actively working for legislation which would outlaw the sale of cigarettes
    d. all of these are part of Mary's attitude toward smoking

33. A car salesman offers to sell a customer a new car for $17,000, which is a very attractive price. After the customer signs the papers to purchase at that price, the salesman seeks final approval from the manager. He returns to tell the customer that the manager will sell the car for $17,700. The customer still agrees to buy. The customer was a victim of

    a. the overjustification effect
    b. low-balling
    c. brainwashing
    d. the door-in-the-face phenomenon

34. Rhonda is more successful in getting her fellow students to donate blood if they first agree to having a bumper sticker advertising the campus blood drive placed on their car. Rhonda's strategy illustrates the

    a. overjustification effect
    b. foot-in-the-door phenomenon
    c. low-ball technique
    d. underjustification effect

35. Nicole loses her interest in playing the piano after her father promises to pay her two dollars for each hour of practice. This illustrates the _____ effect.

    a. insufficient justification
    b. low-ball
    c. overjustification
    d. door-in-the-face

36. Although John is strongly opposed to stricter parking regulations on campus, he is asked to write a paper supporting them. Dissonance theory predicts that his attitude will undergo the most change if he

    a. refuses to write the paper
    b. agrees to write the paper for $200
    c. agrees to write the paper for no pay
    d. refuses to write the paper even after being offered $20

37. Milford has always strongly believed that it is wrong to cheat. But after he cheats on a chemistry quiz, his attitude toward cheating becomes significantly less harsh. What best accounts for this attitude shift?

    a. cognitive dissonance theory
    b. self-perception theory
    c. reinforcement theory
    d. role-playing theory

38. Jennifer had great difficulty deciding whether to attend the local community college or the state university. She finally decided to attend the community college. Dissonance theory predicts that her evaluation of the community college is likely to become more _____ and her evaluation of the state university is likely to become more _____.

    a. positive; positive
    b. positive; negative
    c. negative; positive
    d. negative; negative

39. In which of the following situations would cognitive dissonance theorists predict that the person is experiencing dissonance?

    a. Dan is trying to decide whether to buy a new or used bicycle
    b. Just as Mike finishes mowing the lawn, it begins to rain
    c. Sara has just been accepted into law school
    d. Nancy has just chosen to attend City College rather than State University after receiving equally attractive scholarship offers from both

40. "Let me see, do I like Chinese food? I guess I do because I eat at a Chinese restaurant twice a month." The process reflected in this internal dialogue is best understood in terms of

    a. cognitive dissonance theory
    b. self-perception theory
    c. reinforcement theory
    d. equity theory

SHORT ESSAY QUESTIONS

Answer the following questions in the space provided.

1. Briefly describe the major dimensions of an attitude.

    The major dimensions of attitude are: Affect (feelings), behavior tendency and cognition (thoughts.)

2. What research findings led social psychologists in the 1960s to emphasize the importance of external social influences on behavior?

    That what people say often differs from what they do.

    - *Warnings about smoking affect only minimally those who already smoke.*
    - *Increasing public awareness of the brutalizing effects of tv violence has made many people to desire less violent programming — yet they still watch media murders much as ever.*
    - *Sex education programs 65 influencing attitudes towards abstinence + condom use without affecting long-term abstinence and condom use behavior.*

3. Identify three conditions under which attitudes are likely to predict behavior.

1.) When we minimize other influences upon our attitude statements and our behavior.

2) When the attitude is specifically relevant to the observed behavior.

3.) An attitude predicts a behavior better when the attitude is potent.

4. List four lines of evidence that indicate behavior affects attitude.

- Sarah is hypnotized and told to take her shoes off when a book drops on the floor. Later the book drops she takes her shoes off. When asked why, she says its been a long day, my feet are hot and tired.
- George has electrodes temporarily implanted in his brain region that controls his head movements. When a remote control stimulates his brain, he always turns his head. He responds I was looking for my slipper I'm restless etc.
- Frank, split brain patient, has the word "smile" flashed to his nonverbal right hemisphere. He obliges and forces a smile. When asked why, he explains, this experiment is very funny.

5. How does self-presentation theory explain the effect of our actions on our attitude reports?

6. Briefly compare and contrast self-perception theory and cognitive dissonance theory.

7. Explain the insufficient justification effect and the overjustification effect.

Chapter Review

1. evaluative
   beliefs
   behavior

2. attitudes
   behavior
   behavior
   fail
   external

3. expressed
   outside
   association

4. influences
   relevant
   potent
   automatic
   self-aware

5. think
   act

6. role
   say
   foot-in-the-door

7. Evil
   disparage
   Moral

8. prejudice
   escalation
   participation

9. Self-presentation
   actions

10. dissonance
    decision
    external
    responsible
    dissonance

11. Self-perception
    unsure
    behavior
    overjustification

12. Self-affirmation
    change
    formation

Matching Terms

1. k
2. c
3. i
4. b
5. a
6. g

7. j
8. l
9. d
10. f
11. h
12. e

True-False Review

1. T	14. F
2. F	15. F
3. F	16. T
4. F	17. T
5. T	18. F
6. T	19. F
7. F	20. T
8. T	21. T
9. T	22. F
10. T	23. T
11. F	24. T
12. F	25. F
13. F	

Multiple-Choice Practice Test

1. c	21. c
2. b	22. c
3. d	23. b
4. b	24. d
5. d	25. b
6. b	26. a
7. a	27. c
8. c	28. a
9. c	29. d
10. a	30. a
11. d	31. c
12. b	32. d
13. a	33. b
14. a	34. b
15. a	35. c
16. a	36. c
17. d	37. a
18. b	38. b
19. c	39. d
20. b	40. b

CHAPTER 5

GENES, CULTURE, AND GENDER

CHAPTER OBJECTIVES

After completing your study of this chapter you should be able to:

1. Identify two important perspectives on human similarities and differences.

2. Describe the major themes of evolutionary psychology.

3. Discuss the nature and function of norms.

4. Identify some differing cultural norms and at least one universal norm.

5. Discuss important gender similarities and differences.

6. Explain how the evolutionary psychologist accounts for gender differences, and describe how hormonal differences predispose psychological differences.

7. Discuss how gender roles vary with culture and over time.

8. Describe the relationship between biology and culture, and discuss how persons and situations interact.

CHAPTER REVIEW

Supply the words necessary to complete each of the following statements.

HOW ARE WE INFLUENCED BY HUMAN NATURE AND BY CULTURAL DIVERSITY?

1. Social _____ has become the explosive problem of our time. Two perspectives dominate current thinking on human _____ and _____: the _____ perspective emphasizes human kinship whereas the _____ perspective emphasizes human diversity.

2. Evolutionary psychologists study how _____ selection favors psychological traits that enhance the preservation and spread of one's _____. The evolutionary perspective highlights our _____ human nature.

3. Perhaps our most important similarity, the hallmark of our species, is our capacity to _____ and to adapt. This capacity enables those in one _____ to value promptness and frankness while those in another do not.

4. All cultures have their own norms, or _____ for accepted and expected behavior. Norms restrain and control, but they also _____ the social machinery so that our words and acts come effortlessly. Cultures vary in their norms for expressiveness, punctuality, and _____ space. For reasons unknown, cultures near the equator prefer _____ space, and more touching and hugging.

5. Although cultural norms vary greatly, Roger Brown has described one _____ norm, which concerns how people of unequal _____ relate to one another. We communicate informally with intimates and those of _____ status, and formally with strangers and those of _____ status. Increased _____ is usually initiated by the person with higher status.

6. The best known universal norm is the taboo against _____. Humans even have cross-cultural norms for conducting _____. Some norms are culture-specific, others are universal; we might think of _____ as universal and _____ as culture-specific.

HOW ARE GENDER SIMILARITIES AND DIFFERENCES EXPLAINED?

7. Compared to boys, girls talk more _____ and play less _____. In conversation, men more often than women focus on _____, whereas women focus on personal _____. Women are more likely to describe themselves as having _____ and tend to be better at reading others' _____.

8. In essentially every society, men are socially _____. Research indicates that men also exhibit more physical _____ than women do. There is also a gender gap in _____ attitudes and assertiveness.

EVOLUTION AND GENDER: DOING WHAT COMES NATURALLY?

9. Evolutionary psychologists maintain that natural selection explains males' greater physical _____ and _____ initiative. Men everywhere are attracted to women whose physical features suggest _____. Everywhere, women prefer men with sufficient _____ for nurturing offspring. The gender gap in aggression does seem influenced by the sex hormone _____.

Hormonal changes provide one explanation for why gender differences

_____ with age

CULTURE AND GENDER: DOING AS THE CULTURE SAYS?

10. Behavior _____ for males and females define gender roles. The effect of _____ on gender roles is enormous and is evident from the striking _____ in gender roles throughout the world and across _____. Much of this influence is transmitted via _____.

WHAT CAN WE CONCLUDE ABOUT GENES, CULTURE, AND GENDER?

11. _____ and _____ explanations need not be contradictory. What biology initiates, culture may _____. These two factors also _____ with one another.

12. Power resides in both persons and situations. They _____ in at least three ways. First, individuals vary in how they interpret and _____ to a given situation. Second, people _____ many of the situations that influence them. Third, people help _____ their social situations.

MATCHING TERMS

Write the letter of the term on the right before the appropriate number on the left.

_____ 1. Important vehicle of cultural influence.

_____ 2. A set of behavior expectations for males or females.

_____ 3. Putting oneself in another's shoes.

_____ 4. Predisposes traits that enhance the preservation of one's genes.

_____ 5. They prescribe proper behavior.

_____ 6. The taboo against incest.

_____ 7. Identified a universal norm.

_____ 8. Capable of both assertiveness and nurturance.

_____ 9. The relationship between persons and situations.

_____ 10. A universal dimension of social beliefs.

_____ 11. Social behaviors are subject to natural selection.

_____ 12. Behavior intended to hurt someone.

_____ 13. Characteristics by which people define male and female.

_____ 14. Its size depends on our familiarity with whoever is near us.

a. Brown

b. empathy

c. aggression

d. natural selection

e. androgynous

f. a universal norm

g. gender role

h. evolutionary psychology

i. cynicism

j. gender

k. peers

l. interaction

m. norms

n. personal space

74

TRUE-FALSE REVIEW

Circle T if the statement is true and F if it is false.

T F 1. An evolutionary perspective tends to emphasize our human kinship rather than our diversity.

T F 2. Most people rate their feelings regarding "women" as more favorable than their feelings regarding "men."

T F 3. The portable bubble that we like to maintain between ourselves and others is called a cognitive map.

T F 4. Brown's universal norm is primarily concerned with the way males and females relate to each other.

T F 5. The taboo against incest is a universal norm.

T F 6. Humans have cross-cultural norms for conducting war. .

T F 7. All societies rank people by authority and status.

T F 8. Humans are more genetically varied than are chimps.

T F 9. Latin American business executives who arrive late to dinner may be puzzled by how obsessed their North American counterparts are with punctuality.

T F 10. Among our universal similarities, the hallmark of our species is our capacity to learn and to adapt.

T F 11. In the United States, the male-to-female arrest ratio is 10 to 1.

T F 12. In writing, women use fewer quantitative terms and more present-tense forms.

T F 13. Women tend to be better at reading others' emotions.

T F 14. Across cultures, men tend to marry younger women.

T F 15. National Football League players have higher than normal testosterone levels.

T F 16. In conversation, men tend to interrupt more than do women.

T F 17. Across cultures, males and females are equally likely to initiate sexual relations.

T F 18. Two children in the same family are on average as different from each other as are pairs of children selected randomly from the population.

T F 19. The term *gender role* refers to one's feeling of being a male or female.

T F 20. Compared to males, the average female is less likely to commit suicide or be killed by lightning.

T F 21. If we traced our ancestors back 100,000 or more years, we would see that we are all Africans.

T F 22. In many cultures, boys spend as much time as girls helping with housework and child care.

T F 23. In comparison to men, women in individualist cultures describe themselves in more relational terms and are more attuned to others' relationships.

T F 24. Studies indicate that as men and women grow older, they become more androgynous.

T F 25. One important lesson of social psychology is that persons and situations interact.

MULTIPLE-CHOICE PRACTICE TEST

Circle the correct letter.

1. Norms, according to the text,

    a. are composed of a set of roles
    b. prescribe proper behavior
    c. are social behaviors of typical or average people
    d. are laws that govern the distribution of social rewards

2. Which of the following is true?

    a. there are really no truly universal norms
    b. religion does not exist in some societies
    c. norms can restrain us so subtly that we hardly sense their existence
    d. "fire is hot" is an example of a norm

3. "Personal space" refers to

    a. the property that a person owns, for example, a house and its grounds
    b. the favorite place a person retreats to when privacy is desired
    c. the exact spot that each person occupies, for example, the seats students occupy in a classroom
    d. the buffer zone that people like to maintain around their bodies

4. The cultural perspective highlights the importance of _____ in explaining the diversity of languages, customs, and expressive behaviors across the world.

   a. natural selection
   b. role playing
   c. hormonal factors
   d. human adaptability

5. Roger Brown's "universal norm" is

   a. the incest taboo
   b. the fact that we relate to people of higher status the way we do to strangers, and to people of lower status the way we do to intimate friends
   c. the fact that people the world over tend to relate to people of inferior status in the ways they relate to strangers
   d. the prohibition of theft

6. The enduring behaviors, ideas, attitudes, and traditions shared by a large group of people and transmitted from one generation to the next defines

   a. social roles
   b. role diffusion
   c. ingroup bias
   d. a culture

7. Studies of twins and biological and adoptive siblings indicate that genetic influences explain roughly _____ of individual variations in personality traits.

   a. 30
   b. 50
   c. 70
   d. 90

8. If a genetically based fear of wild animals contributes to survival, that trait will likely be passed on to subsequent generations. This best illustrates

   a. Brown's universal norm
   b. an emergent norm
   c. hormonal influence
   d. natural selection

9. Which of the following friendship norms seems to be universal?

   a. Be prompt in keeping appointments with a friend
   b. Respect your friend's privacy
   c. Help your friend find a suitable spouse
   d. Ask a friend's opinion before making a major decision

10. Cross-cultural studies of sexual behaviors indicate that

    a. with few exceptions males are more likely than females to initiate sexual relations
    b. in most societies males and females are equally likely to initiate sexual relations
    c. in societies where females outnumber males, females initiate sexual relations
    d. in third-world countries females are more likely than males are to initiate sexual relations

11. The study of how natural selection predisposes adaptive traits and behavior is called

    a. behavioral genetics   c. evolutionary psychology
    b. biological behaviorism   d. genetic psychology

12. Research indicates that a gender difference exists in

    a. vocabulary   c. age at which infants walk
    b. intelligence   d. smiling

13. According to Alice Eagly and Wendy Wood, biology and culture contribute to sex differences in behavior

    a. by influencing the roles people play
    b. by directly determining the personal traits of males and females
    c. through the process of natural selection
    d. by influencing the verbal and nonverbal communication styles of males and females

14. In essentially every known society,

    a. men are socially dominant
    b. men are more verbally fluent
    c. there are more male than female physicians
    d. males are responsible for finding enough food to eat

15. Critics have suggested that evolutionary psychology is characterized by

    a. the base-rate fallacy
    b. counterfactual thinking
    c. hindsight bias
    d. regression toward the average

16. _____ is more common in males than in females.

    a. Anxiety   c. Empathy
    b. Depression   d. ADHD

17. A noticeable difference has not been found between males and females in

    a. happiness
    b. judging emotion on people's faces
    c. suicide rate
    d. frequency of smiling

18. According to evolutionary psychologists, which of the following is most fundamental to understanding the development of social behavior?

    a. cultural norms   c. natural selection
    b. hormonal factors   d. brain organization

19. Research on possible hormonal influences on aggression has indicated that

    a. testosterone levels influence animal aggression but not human aggression
    b. violent male criminals have higher than normal testosterone levels
    c. gender differences in aggression are clearly unrelated to hormonal differences
    d. administering testosterone reduces aggression in most animals

20. Which of the following groups maintains the least personal space?

    a. British   c. Arabs
    b. Americans   d. Scandinavians

21. Research on gender differences suggests that _____ are better at reading others' emotions and that _____ are better at expressing emotions nonverbally.

    a. women; women   c. men; women
    b. women; men   d. men; men

22. A set of behavior expectations for males or females is a

    a. gender norm   c. gender assignment
    b. sex-role preference   d. gender role

23. Recent surveys in the United States suggest that, compared to women, men are more likely to support

    a. liberal political candidates
    b. the use of capital punishment
    c. programs that preserve and promote group equality
    d. female political candidates

24. According to the text, which of the following is true of the biological and cultural perspectives?

    a. Biological and cultural factors are independent of each other
    b. Biological and cultural perspectives are contradictory
    c. Biological and cultural factors interact
    d. Biological and cultural perspectives are identical

25. Research on conversational styles indicates that

    a. men's and women's conversational styles vary with the social context
    b. women are more fluent than men
    c. women are more likely to use the active than passive voice
    d. men and women are from different planets

26. Survey research indicates that _____ percent of scientists believe that "human beings have developed over millions of years" and that _____ percent of Americans believe that "human beings developed from earlier species."

    a   95; 38   c.   75; 12
    b. 98; 65   d.   68; 56

27. Studies indicate that girls who are exposed to excess _____ during fetal development tend to exhibit more tomboyish play behavior.

    a. estrogen   c.   testosterone
    b. glucose   d.   endorphins

28. Which of the following is not one of the universal dimensions of social beliefs that are applied in daily life?

    a. empathy   c.   spirituality
    b. cynicism   d.   fate control

29. Research in developmental psychology indicates that

    a. genetic influences explain about 70 percent of our individual variations in personality traits
    b. siblings are as different from one another as are pairs of children selected randomly from the population
    c. the home is the most important influence in shaping a child's personality traits
    d. children and youth learn their games, musical tastes, and even their dirty words mostly from their siblings

30. Which of the following statements is true of the relationship between persons and situations?

    a. A given situation affects different people differently
    b. People choose many of their situations
    c. People help create the situations that affect them
    d. All of these are true

31. As people mature to middle age and beyond,

    a. both men and women become increasingly androgynous
    b. women but not men become increasingly androgynous
    c. men but not women become increasingly androgynous
    d. both men and women become decreasingly androgynous

32. In response to the question, "Do you think it is wrong for unmarried couples to bear children?" a 1997 World Gallup poll reported that

    a. the majority of people in all cultures surveyed said "yes"
    b. a minority of people in all cultures surveyed said "yes"
    c. about half the people in each culture surveyed said "yes"
    d. the percentage of people who said "yes" varied enormously from culture to culture

33. On visits to other countries, you would be most likely to observe men and women involved equally

    a. as legislators
    b. in child care
    c. in cooking and dishwashing
    d. in planting and harvesting crops

34. Which of the following statements illustrates Roger Brown's "universal norm"?

    a. Brothers do not have sexual relations with their sisters in Daneria
    b. The King of Sindab invites subjects to his castle for dinner before they invite him to their huts for dinner
    c. Friends in Transylvania do not divulge things said in confidence
    d. Males rather than females initiate sexual relations in Wallonia

35. William is gentle and affectionate with his children but independent and assertive in running his business. Which term best describes his personality?

    a. androgynous   c. gender schematic
    b. gender diffused   d. interrole patterned

36. "Drivers are expected to keep to the right on a two-lane road" is an example of what the text calls a

    a. norm   c. position
    b. role   d. status

37. When Jermaine falls off his bicycle, he does not cry because he has learned that boys are not expected to. Jermaine's behavior best illustrates the significance of

    a. natural selection
    b. gender roles
    c. the universal belief of fate control
    d. testosterone

38. The evolutionary perspective is to the cultural perspective as _____ is to _____.

    a. gender role; social role
    b. coevolution; empathy
    c. role; norm
    d. human kinship; human diversity

39. Research suggests that 12-year-old Rafael is most likely to become a smoker if

    a. his parents smoke
    b. his friends smoke
    c. his brothers smoke
    d. his sisters smoke

40. In terms of the process of gender socialization, girls are to _____ as boys are to _____.

    a. legs; arms
    b. flowers; stems
    c. bread; butter
    d. roots; wings

SHORT ESSAY QUESTIONS

Answer the following questions in the space provided.

1. Contrast the evolutionary and cultural perspectives on human similarities and differences.

2. Define *norm* and give one specific example of how norms vary by culture.

3. Describe Roger Brown's universal norm.

4. Discuss three important gender differences.

5. Discuss the evolutionary psychologist's perspective on gender differences.

6. Describe how gender roles vary with culture and over time.

7. What conclusion does the text reach regarding the relationship between biological and cultural influences?

8. Describe three ways in which persons and situations interact.

ANSWER KEY

Chapter Review

1. diversity
   similarities
   differences
   evolutionary
   cultural

2. natural
   genes
   universal

3. learn
   culture

4. standards
   grease
   personal
   less

5. universal
   status
   lower
   higher
   intimacy

6. incest
   war
   nature
   nurture

7. intimately
   aggressively
   tasks
   relationships
   empathy
   emotions

8. dominant
   aggression
   sexual

9. aggression
   sexual
   fertility
   resources
   testosterone
   shrink

10. expectations
    culture
    variations
    time
    peers

11. Biological
    cultural
    accentuate
    interact

12. interact
    react
    choose
    create

Matching Terms

1. k
2. g
3. b
4. d
5. m
6. f
7. a

8. e
9. l
10. i
11. h
12. c
13. j
14. n

True-False Review

1.	T	14.	T
2.	T	15.	T
3.	F	16.	T
4.	F	17.	F
5.	T	18.	T
6.	T	19.	F
7.	T	20.	T
8.	F	21.	T
9.	T	22.	F
10.	T	23.	T
11.	T	24.	T
12.	T	25.	T
13.	T		

Multiple-Choice Practice Test

1.	b	21.	a
2.	c	22.	d
3.	d	23.	b
4.	d	24.	c
5.	b	25.	a
6.	d	26.	a
7.	b	27.	c
8.	d	28.	a
9.	b	29.	b
10.	a	30.	d
11.	c	31.	a
12.	d	32.	d
13.	a	33.	d
14.	a	34.	b
15.	c	35.	a
16.	d	36.	a
17.	a	37.	b
18.	c	38.	d
19.	b	39.	b
20.	c	40.	d

CHAPTER 6

CONFORMITY AND OBEDIENCE

CHAPTER OBJECTIVES

After completing your study of this chapter you should be able to:

1. Define conformity and explain the difference between "compliance" and "acceptance."

2. Describe the findings of the classic conformity and obedience studies.

3. Identify circumstances that are conducive to conformity.

4. Explain why people conform.

5. Indicate how personality, cultural background, and social roles are related to conformity.

6. Explain why people sometimes resist social pressure.

CHAPTER REVIEW

Supply the words necessary to complete each of the following statements.

WHAT IS CONFORMITY?
1. Conformity is a change in _____ or _____ as the result of real or imagined group pressure.
2. Conformity comes in two forms: _____ is publicly acting in accord with an implied or explicit request while privately disagreeing. _____ is both acting and believing in accord with social pressure. _____ is acting in accord with a direct command.

WHAT ARE THE CLASSIC CONFORMITY AND OBEDIENCE STUDIES?
3. Sherif found that estimates of the _____ phenomenon, the apparent movement of a stationary point of light in the dark, were easily influenced by

the _____ of others. The group _____ lasted over long periods of time and succeeding generations of subjects.

4. Asch had individuals listen to other people estimate which of three comparison _____ matched the standard. Although the others gave an obviously _____ response, participants conformed 37 percent of the time.

5. Milgram investigated the degree to which people would obey an authority's instructions to deliver what were presumably traumatizing _____ _____ to another person in an adjacent room. Under optimum conditions—a _____, close-at-hand commander, a _____ victim, and no one else to exemplify disobedience—65 percent of adult male participants fully complied.

6. The conformity studies illustrate at least three social-psychological principles discussed in earlier chapters: The impact of behavior on _____, the power of the _____ to shape action, and the _____ attribution error.

WHAT PREDICTS CONFORMITY?

7. Conformity is influenced by several characteristics of the group. It is highest when the group is composed of _____ or more persons, is unanimous in its judgment, is cohesive, and is high in _____.

8. People also conform more when their responses are _____ and when they have not previously _____ themselves to a particular position.

WHY CONFORM?

9. People conform for two reasons: _____ influence is based on a person's desire to fulfill others' expectations, often to gain acceptance. _____ influence is conformity that results from accepting evidence about reality provided by other people.

WHO CONFORMS?

10. Researchers in the 1980s found that personality traits predict social behaviors such as conformity when measured across many _____. Personality also predicts behavior when social influences are _____. _____ differences in conformity suggest that people can be socialized to be more or less socially responsive. Social _____ require a certain degree of conformity.

DO WE EVER WANT TO BE DIFFERENT?

11. Blatant attempts at social coercion produce _____—a motive to protect or restore one's sense of freedom. Reactance may contribute to the problem of underage _____.

12. People are uncomfortable when they appear too different from others, but neither do they want to appear the _____ as everyone else. Thus they will often act to preserve their sense of _____ and individuality.

MATCHING TERMS

Write the letter of the correct term on the right before the appropriate number on the left.

_____ 1. A "we feeling"—the extent to which members of a group are bound together, such as by attraction for one another.

_____ 2. Conformity that results from accepting evidence about reality provided by other people.

_____ 3. A motive to protect or preserve one's sense of freedom.

_____ 4. Most people indicate their distinctive attributes.

_____ 5. The apparent movement of a stationary point of light in a dark room.

_____ 6. Studied obedience to authority.

_____ 7. A change in behavior or belief to accord with others.

_____ 8. Social contagion produced by a face-rubbing or foot-shaking person.

_____ 9. The underestimation of social forces.

_____ 10. Happy people help us feel happier.

_____ 11. Used judgments of the lengths of lines to study conformity.

_____ 12. Conformity based on a person's desire to fulfill others' expectations, often to gain acceptance.

_____ 13. Used the autokinetic phenomenon to study conformity.

a. conformity

b. Sherif

c. autokinetic phenomenon

d. mood linkage

e. Asch

f. the chameleon effect

g. Milgram

h. cohesiveness

i. normative influence

j informational influence

k. fundamental attribution error

l. reactance

m. spontaneous self-concept

TRUE-FALSE REVIEW

Circle T if the statement is true and F if it is false.

T F   1. Conformity is sometimes good and sometimes bad.

T F   2. Compliance and acceptance are different forms of conformity.

T F   3. Fatal auto accidents and private airplane crashes increase after well-publicized suicides.

T F   4. A confederate who made an inflated estimate of the autokinetic phenomenon had no effect on the judgments of naive participants.

T F   5. In Asch's study involving the judgment of length of lines, the correct answer was obvious.

T F   6. Asch's experimental procedure had "mundane" but not "experimental" realism.

T F   7. People comply more with requests from those they believe share their birthday.

T F   8. Milgram found that a total of 37 percent of male participants fully complied with the experimenter's commands.

T F   9. When Milgram's experiment was repeated in a modest commercial building in Bridgeport, the percent of the participants who fully complied to the commands of the experimenter remained unchanged.

T F   10. In the Milgram obedience studies, people of lower status tended to accept the experimenter's commands more readily than did people of higher status.

T F   11. When surveyed afterward, most of Milgram's participants said they regretted having volunteered to participate in his study.

T F   12. Compliance can breed acceptance.

T F   13. The conformity research indicates that evil has its basis in a human character defect.

T F   14. In experiments on decision making by simulated juries, hung verdicts are more likely when jurors are polled by a show of hands rather than by secret ballot.

T F   15. Two groups of three people elicit more conformity than one group of six.

T F   16. Group members who feel attracted to the group are more responsive to the group's influence than are groups members who are less attracted to the group.

T F 17. After university women gave some thought to how traditional culture expects women to behave, they became more likely to exhibit traditional feminine modesty.

T F 18. People conform more when they must respond in the presence of others than when allowed to write down their answers privately.

T F 19. Normative social influence results from a person's desire to find meaning in life.

T F 20. Given a light touch on the arm, people are more likely to lend a dime or sample a new pizza.

T F 21. Replications of Asch's experiment in Britain, Canada, and the United States typically trigger more conformity than Asch observed two or three decades earlier.

T F 22. Knowing people's cultural backgrounds helps us predict how conforming they are.

T F 23. In Japan, going along with others is a sign of maturity.

T F 24. The theory of psychological reactance states that people desire consistency in their lives.

T F 25. When people are asked, "Tell us about yourself," they are most likely to report characteristics they share in common with others.

MULTIPLE-CHOICE PRACTICE TEST

Circle the correct letter.

1. _____ is a change in behavior or belief to accord with others.

    a. Cohesiveness   c. Compliance
    b. Conformity   d. Obedience

2. Publicly acting in accord with an implied or explicit request while privately disagreeing is called

    a. acceptance   c. reactance
    b. compliance   d. interaction

3. Both acting and believing in accord with social pressure is called

    a. acceptance   c. compliance
    b. reactance   d. interaction

4. An important difference between Asch's experiment in which participants judged the length of lines and Sherif's experiment in which participants judged the movement of light was that

   a Asch's participants were older than were Sherif's
   b. there was an obviously correct answer in judging the length of lines but not in judging the movement of light
   c. Asch's participants made their judgments privately whereas Sherif's participants made their judgments publicly
   d. Asch's participants were all male whereas Sherif's participants were both male and female

5. In Asch's study of perceptual judgment involving the length of lines, naive participants conformed _____ of the time to the false judgments of the confederates.

   a. 10 percent   c. 68 percent
   b. 37 percent   d. 92 percent

6. In using the autokinetic phenomenon, Jacobs and Campbell found that when a confederate gave an inflated estimate of how far the light moved

   a. naive participants were not influenced by the confederate's estimate
   b. naive participants who heard the estimate were influenced but new members who joined were not
   c. the confederate's judgment not only had an immediate influence but the inflated illusion also persisted for five generations
   d. the confederate's judgment had no immediate influence on group members but did have a delayed effect by shaping the estimates of group members after they left the group

7. Studies involving _____ most clearly demonstrate social influence taking the form of acceptance.

   a. the "boomerang effect"
   b. judgments of the autokinetic phenomenon
   c. shocking innocent victims
   d. administration of a drug overdose

8. Participants' tendencies to obey the experimenter's commands to shock a victim were highest when the experimenter was _____ and the victim was
   _____.

   a. close; distant   c. distant; distant
   b. close; close   d. distant; close

9. When the study of obedience was moved from Yale University to Bridgeport, Connecticut, the number of people who complied

   a. decreased from 65 percent to 48 percent
   b. decreased from 75 percent to 25 percent
   c. increased from 37 percent to 50 percent
   d. decreased from 37 percent to 10 percent

10. In a Pennsylvania State University experiment in which students were asked to predict how they would respond to a male's sexist comments, a _____ of students said they would ignore them. When other students actually heard such sexist remarks being made, a _____ of students said nothing.

   a. minority; minority   c. majority; minority
   b. minority; majority   d. majority; majority

11. A psychiatrist who interviewed 40 of Milgram's participants a year after their participation concluded that

   a. none had been harmed
   b. many were suspicious of all authorities
   c. a minority had lowered self-esteem
   d. most regretted having served in Milgram's study

12. When hospital nurses were called by an unknown physician and ordered to administer an obvious overdose of a drug,

   a. the majority of nurses did not comply and reported the incident to their supervisor
   b. the inexperienced nurses complied whereas the more experienced ones challenged the order
   c. most indicated to the physician that he would have to come in to sign the order before they could comply
   d. all but one proceeded to comply without delay

13. Which of the following social-psychological principles is not illustrated by the conformity literature?

   a. behavior shapes attitudes
   b. the fundamental attribution error
   c. the inoculation effect
   d. the power of the situation

14. To believe that Asch's compliant participants were particularly spineless people is to

    a. forget that behavior shapes belief
    b. overlook other personality characteristics that determine conformity
    c. make the fundamental attribution error
    d. ignore how the status of the experimenter shapes behavior

15. How social pressure may lead us to perform immoral acts is best illustrated by studies of

    a. psychological reactance   c. obedience to authority
    b. spontaneous self-concept   d. informational influence

16. Increasing the size of the group from _____ to _____ is likely to produce the greatest increase in conformity.

    a. 1000 to 2000   c. 2 to 5
    b. 50 to 100   d. 5 to 10

17. According to the text, suggestibility on a mass scale was evident in

    a. the wave of flying saucer sightings in the late 1940s
    b. the "ethnic cleansings" occurring in Iraq and Bosnia
    c. the use of torture by the military junta in Greece during the early 1970s
    d. Le Chambon's sheltering of the Jews during the Holocaust

18. Conformity is highest when the response is _____ and _____.

    a. private; made without prior commitment
    b. public; made without prior commitment
    c. nonverbal; made in response to inanimate objects
    d. insignificant; made with prior commitment

19. Milgram reported that a participant's tendency to obey the experimenter decreased dramatically

    a. when two other participants defied the experimenter
    b. when the participant could not hear the responses of the learner
    c. when the experimenter was a female
    d. when the experimenter was younger than the participant

20. The training of torturers by the military junta in Greece in the early 1970s illustrates

    a. psychological reactance
    b. the inoculation effect
    c. the foot-in-the-door phenomenon
    d. the role of personality in conformity

21. Normative influence is to informational influence as _____ is to
    _____.

    a. autokinetic effect; cohesiveness
    b. compliance; acceptance
    c. conformity; reactance
    d. acceptance; reactance

22. _____ is based on a person's desire to be correct.

    a. Indirect influence   c. Normative influence
    b. Nominal influence   d. Informational influence

23. _____ is based on a person's desire to be accepted by the group.

    a. Indirect influence   c. Normative influence
    b. Nominal influence   d. Informational influence

24. Which of the following is true regarding individual differences in conformity?

    a. Obedience rates in Austria and Italy are much lower than in the United States
    b. French participants conform less than Norwegian participants
    c. People's self-esteem test scores are excellent predictors of conformity
    d. American participants conform slightly more than German participants

25. The case of Patty Hearst illustrates

    a. the powerful effect of role playing
    b. how conformity can be constructive
    c. the strong need to be unique
    d. cultural differences in conformity and independence

26. Psychological reactance theory provides an explanation for

    a. resistance to authority
    b. obedience to authority
    c. why compliance is more common than acceptance
    d. why people are most likely to conform when the group is unanimous

27. In studying the impact of a confederate who occasionally rubbed her face or shook her foot,
    Tanya Chartrand and John Bargh found evidence of

    a. reactance   c. a chameleon effect
    b. normative social influence   d. the fundamental attribution error

28. Studies of people's spontaneous self-concepts indicate that

    a. people see themselves as better than average
    b. people react to blatant social pressure
    c. females define themselves in terms of their similarities whereas males define themselves in terms of their differences
    d. people value their uniqueness

29. Research has indicated that the number of suicides increases following

    a. well-publicized suicides
    b. a world war
    c. the Olympic games
    d. an economic recession

30. When Asch's conformity experiment was repeated in other countries, the highest rate of conformity was found in

    a. Lebanon
    b. the Bantu of Zimbabwe
    c. Hong Kong
    d. Brazil

31. According to the text, constructive conformity was evident in

    a. restaurant managers complying with orders from a phone caller posing as a police officer
    b. heroic firefighters rushing into the flaming World Trade Center
    c. undergraduate students yawning in response to a boring speaker
    d. the Seattle windshield pitting epidemic

32. People who observed a lone individual in a group of four misjudge blue stimuli as green were subsequently

    a. more likely to conform to a group's erroneous judgments
    b. less likely to conform to a group's erroneous judgments
    c. less likely to value individualism
    d. more likely to value wisdom

33. After hearing a respected medical authority lecture about the value of eating fresh fruits and vegetables, Joshua includes more of them in his diet. This change in Joshua's eating patterns is an example of

    a. normative social influence
    b. psychological reactance
    c. informational social influence
    d. social facilitation

34. Peter hates to wear ties anywhere. Nevertheless he wears one to his sister's wedding to avoid the disapproval of his family. This is an example of

    a. identification
    b. informational social influence
    c. normative social influence
    d. psychological reactance

35. Ancient astronomers who observed the stars occasionally saw a star that seemed to move abruptly. This is probably an example of

    a. the autokinetic effect   c. astronomical impact theory
    b. the inoculation effect   d. normative social influence

36. In light of the Milgram studies, to believe that soldiers who shoot innocent civilians as a consequence of following orders are unusually cruel is to

    a. make the fundamental attribution error
    b. engage in self-serving bias
    c. overlook the effect of cultural differences on conformity
    d. underestimate the influence of personality differences on conformity

37. Philip hates to attend concerts but goes because his wife wants to. After three years, Philip comes to genuinely enjoy concerts. This is an example of

    a. how acceptance can lead to compliance
    b. how compliance can lead to acceptance
    c. the "boomerang effect"
    d. how psychological reactance can lead to acceptance

38. Presidents rarely shift their positions on major foreign policy matters. This may be an example of how

    a. a "we-they" feeling has emerged between the major political parties
    b. public commitment reduces susceptibility to social influence
    c. high self-esteem is strongly related to nonconformity
    d. emotional distance from victims leads to disregard for their welfare

39. Milly generally likes to go home to visit her family during vacation. However, after her father tells her she must be home during spring vacation, Milly decides to remain at college. We can probably best understand Milly's behavior in terms of

    a. reaction formation   c. psychological reactance
    b. regression   d. self-serving bias

40. John has red hair, has two brothers, one sister, and was born in Chicago. Both his parents were born in this country and are lawyers. If you asked John to "tell us about yourself," he is most likely to mention that

    a. he has two brothers   c. his father has a college education
    b. he has red hair   d. he was born in this country

SHORT ESSAY QUESTIONS

Answer the following questions in the space provided.

1. Define *conformity*. Explain the distinction between compliance and acceptance.

2. Briefly describe how each of the following investigators attempted to study conformity.

   A. Sherif

   B. Asch

   C. Milgram

3. Identify three factors that are important to understanding <u>when</u> people conform.

4. Give two reasons <u>why</u> people conform.

5. Identify two personal characteristics that are important to understanding <u>who</u> conforms.

6. Give two reasons why people sometimes resist influence.

ANSWER KEY

Chapter Review

1. behavior
   belief

2. Compliance
   Acceptance
   Obedience

3. autokinetic
   estimates
   norm

4. lines
   incorrect

5. electric shocks
   legitimate
   remote

6. attitudes
   situation
   fundamental

7. three
   status

8. public
   committed

9. Normative
   Informational

10. situations
    weak
    Cultural
    roles

11. reactance
    drinking

12. same
    uniqueness

Matching Terms

1.	h	8.	f
2.	j	9.	k
3.	l	10.	d
4.	m	11.	e
5.	c	12.	i
6.	g	13.	b
7.	a		

True-False Review

1.	T	14.	T
2.	T	15.	T
3.	T	16.	T
4.	F	17.	F
5.	T	18.	T
6.	F	19.	F
7.	T	20.	T
8.	F	21.	F
9.	F	22.	T
10.	T	23.	T
11.	F	24.	F
12.	T	25.	F
13.	F		

Multiple-Choice Practice Test

1.	b	21.	b
2.	b	22.	d
3.	a	23.	c
4.	b	24.	b
5.	b	25.	a
6.	c	26.	a
7.	b	27.	c
8.	a	28.	d
9.	a	29.	a
10.	b	30.	b
11.	a	31.	b
12.	d	32.	b
13.	c	33.	c
14.	c	34.	c
15.	c	35.	a
16.	c	36.	a
17.	a	37.	b
18.	b	38.	b
19.	a	39.	c
20.	c	40.	b

CHAPTER 7

PERSUASION

After completing your study of this chapter you should be able to:

1. Identify the two paths to persuasion.

2. Describe communicator characteristics that contribute to effective communication.

3. Explain how the content of the message influences its effectiveness.

4. Describe the effects of different channels of communication.

5. Identify characteristics of the audience that influence susceptibility to persuasion.

6. Discuss the persuasion principles utilized in cult indoctrination.

7. Explain how people may resist persuasion.

CHAPTER REVIEW

Supply the words necessary to complete each of the following statements.

WHAT PATHS LEAD TO PERSUASION?
1. Central route persuasion occurs when interested people focus on the
   _____ and respond with favorable _____. Peripheral
   route persuasion occurs when people are influenced by incidental _____
   such as a speaker's _____.

WHAT ARE THE ELEMENTS OF PERSUASION?

2. The four factors extensively studied in research on persuasion have been the _____, the message, _____ the message is communicated, and the _____.

3. Credible communicators are both _____ and _____. People who speak _____ and look listeners straight in the eye are viewed as more credible. Trustworthiness is also increased if the audience believes the communicator is not trying to persuade them, argues against his or her own _____, and _____ fast.

4. _____ communicators, for example, those with physical appeal or who are similar to the audience, are also persuasive. Similar communicators are more effective on matters of personal _____ than on judgments of _____.

5. Messages are more convincing when associated with _____ _____. Messages that arouse _____ can also be effective especially when the listener is given effective ways to reduce it.

6. The effect of _____ depends on the communicator's credibility. Highly credible people elicit the most opinion change when they argue a relatively _____ position. Less credible people are more successful advocating a _____ position. Those highly _____ in an issue tend to accept a narrow range of views.

7. A one-sided appeal is more effective than a two-sided appeal when the audience _____ with the message and is _____ of opposing arguments.

8. In terms of arguments being presented first or last, the most common finding has been a _____ effect. However, when _____ separates the two messages and if a _____ must be made immediately after hearing the second side, a _____ effect is more likely.

9. Attitudes developed from active _____ are stronger than those shaped by appeals passively received. Although the mass media are typically not as potent as _____ influence, the media are effective when the issue is minor or _____. Many of the media's effects operate in a " _____ flow" of communication—from media to _____ leaders to the rank and file.

10. People with _____ self-esteem are the easiest to influence. The _____ of the audience is also important. We seem to form our basic attitudes when young and carry them through adulthood.

11. What the audience is _____ while listening to a message determines its impact. _____ an audience of a disagreeable message reduces persuasion by stimulating _____. In contrast, _____ people while they hear a disagreeable message can increase _____ by interfering with counterarguing.

EXTREME PERSUASION: HOW DO CULTS INDOCTRINATE?

12. Cults strengthen members' commitment by utilizing the principle that compliance breeds _____. By gradually increasing demands, the cult exploits the _____ phenomenon.

13. Successful cults have a _____ leader and present a vivid, _____ message that is directed to people who are at a _____ point in their lives. The cult typically _____ members in like-minded groups.

HOW CAN PERSUASION BE RESISTED?

14. A prior public _____ to one's position, stimulated perhaps by a _____ attack on the position, breeds resistance to later persuasion. The attack on one's belief stimulates one to develop _____ that immunize against further attacks.

MATCHING TERMS

Write the letter of the term on the right before the appropriate number on the left.

_____ 1. Information presented first has the most influence.

_____ 2. Breeds counterarguing.

_____ 3. Produced by weak attacks on people's beliefs.

_____ 4. The impact of a noncredible person may increase over time.

_____ 5. Influential on matters of personal value.

_____ 6. Especially effective when coupled with specific recommendations.

_____ 7. Isolation from family and friends produces this.

_____ 8. Information presented last has the most influence.

_____ 9. How the media influence the rank and file.

_____ 10. Face-to-face, in writing, on film.

_____ 11. Occurs when people are influenced by incidental cues.

_____ 12. Determines the effect of "discrepant" messages.

_____ 13. Marshals systematic arguments to stimulate favorable thinking.

_____ 14. Process by which a message induces change in beliefs, attitudes, or behaviors.

a. sleeper effect

b. fear appeals

c. primacy effect

d. recency effect

e. communication channels

f. central route persuasion

g. attitude inoculation

h. communicator's credibility

i. persuasion

j. peripheral route persuasion

k. forewarning

l. two-step flow

m. similar communicators

n. social implosion

TRUE-FALSE REVIEW

Circle T if the statement is true and F if it is false.

T F 1. According to the text, health promotion campaigns have helped to decrease the rate of smoking in Canada.

T F 2. Studies of political polls and primary election voting indicate that candidates benefit from being listed first.

T F 3. The term *sleeper effect* refers to the fact that what people are doing when a message is presented influences its effectiveness.

T F 4. Speakers who talk rapidly are generally seen as lacking in credibility.

T F 5. The central route to persuasion is best illustrated by advertisements that feature Hollywood stars.

T F 6. Dissimilar communicators are more effective than similar communicators on matters of objective reality.

T F 7. Communicators are viewed as more trustworthy if the audience believes they are not trying to persuade them.

T F 8. Researchers found that college students were more convinced by persuasive messages if allowed to enjoy peanuts and Pepsi while reading them.

T F 9. Fear-framed messages work better when constructed to promote the prevention of a bad outcome (such as cancer) rather than the promotion of a good outcome (such as fitness).

T F 10. Well-educated audiences are more responsive to rational appeals than are less-educated audiences.

T F 11. In comparison to the peripheral route, the central route to persuasion is more likely to lead to lasting attitude and behavioral change.

T F 12. When people's attitudes were formed primarily through emotion, they are more persuaded by intellectual rather than emotional appeals.

T F 13. A highly credible source elicits most opinion change by advocating a position moderately discrepant from the position held by the recipient.

T F 14. Two-sided arguments are more effective than one-sided arguments if the listener initially disagrees with the communicator's position.

T F 15. In terms of the order of arguments, a recency effect is more commonly found than a primacy effect.

T F 16. Television advertisements for aspirin are generally ineffective.

T F 17. Cult influence techniques are in some ways similar to techniques used by more familiar groups.

T F 18. Messages are best comprehended and recalled when written.

T F 19. The "two-step flow of communication" model has been used to explain the mass media's effect on the audience.

T F 20. Forewarning people that they will be exposed to a discrepant message reduces their susceptibility to it.

T F 21. The life-cycle explanation offers the best account of the generation gap.

T F 22. Cult leaders use the foot-in-the-door technique to gain behavior commitments.

T F 23. The group isolation that occurs in cults leads to "social implosion."

T F 24. "Attitude inoculation" is accomplished by offering people new arguments to bolster their existing attitudes.

T F 25. Being an active listener may build up one's resistance to persuasion.

MULTIPLE-CHOICE PRACTICE TEST

Circle the letter of the correct answer.

1. According to the text, the power of persuasion is evident in Americans'

    a. increased use of seat belts   c. decreased rate of cigarette smoking
    b. decreased rate of obesity   d. increased rate of exercise

2. The central route is to _____ as the peripheral route is to _____.

    a. analytical; motivated
    b. similarity; attractiveness
    c. heuristics; incidental cues
    d. high effort; low effort

3. Social psychologists study persuasion primarily through

    a. experiments
    b. surveys
    c. case studies
    d. participant observation

4. Credible communicators are both _____ and _____.

    a. expert; attractive
    b. intelligent; mature
    c. attractive; intelligent
    d. expert; trustworthy

5. Communicators who talk fast and look the listener in the eye are likely to be perceived as more

    a. selfish
    b. manipulative
    c. attractive
    d. credible

6. Which of the following is one of the four major factors studied by psychologists in research on effective persuasion?

    a. function of communication
    b. setting of communication
    c. channel of communication
    d. length of communication

7. Which of the following statements most clearly demonstrates the "sleeper effect"?

    a. Unsuspecting people often fail to distinguish education from propaganda
    b. A foreign language can be acquired by listening to records while one sleeps
    c. The impact of a noncredible person may increase over time
    d. People who are not alert rarely counterargue

8. Fear-framed messages work better when they are constructed to _____ rather than to _____.

    a. persuade children; persuade adults
    b. persuade adults; persuade children
    c. prevent a bad outcome (such as cancer); promote a good outcome (such as fitness)
    d. promote a good outcome (such as fitness); prevent a bad outcome (such as cancer)

9. People who argue against their own self-interest

   a. are effective in persuading a female audience but not in persuading a male audience
   b. are effective with an intelligent audience but not with an unintelligent audience
   c. are viewed as inconsistent and thus lose their effectiveness
   d. are viewed as more credible and are thus more influential

10. "Similar" communicators are more effective in persuading on _____ than on _____.

    a. radio; television
    b. judgments of fact; matters of value
    c. political issues; religious beliefs
    d. matters of value; judgments of fact

11. Research indicates that stimulating audience members' thinking makes strong messages _____ persuasive and weak messages _____ persuasive.

    a. more; more
    b. more; less
    c. less; more
    d. less; less

12. Robert Cialdini and colleagues' use of the "poison parasite" defense to resist persuasion combines

    a. strong counterarguments with retrieval cues that bring those arguments to mind
    b. forewarning with the foot-in-the-door phenomenon
    c. a highly credible communicator with a highly charismatic appeal
    d. attitude inoculation with social implosion

13. The text suggests that the powers of persuasion were apparent in what a Pew survey called the "rift" between

    a. conservatives and liberals over antipoverty programs
    b. Americans and Western Europeans over the Iraq war
    c. white and black Americans over affirmative action
    d. Israelis and Arabs over the issue of terrorism

14. Which factor has been shown to influence the impact a discrepant message has on the audience?

    a. age of the audience   c. communicator credibility
    b. communication channel   d. communicator attractiveness

15. American World War II soldiers initially opposed to a message suggesting that the Japanese would not be easily defeated were more persuaded by a _____ communication. Soldiers initially agreeing with the message were strengthened more by a _____ message.

    a. videotaped; written
    b. one-sided; two-sided
    c. emotional; rational
    d. two-sided; one-sided

16. When two persuasive messages are presented back to back and the audience responds at some later time,

    a. a primacy effect occurs
    b. a recency effect occurs
    c. a primacy effect occurs with rational appeals, but a recency effect occurs with emotional appeals
    d. social implosion occurs

17. Persuasion studies have shown that the major influence on our most important beliefs and attitudes is

    a. television and radio
    b. the school
    c. the church
    d. our contact with people

18. Highly credible communicators elicit most opinion change when they advocate positions that

    a. differ only moderately from the position of the audience
    b. differ extensively from the position of the audience
    c. elicit strong reactance from the audience
    d. arouse strong dissonance in the audience

19. The mass media's persuasive power is most noticeable on

    a. religious beliefs
    b. matters of objective fact
    c. political values
    d. minor or unfamiliar issues

20. The results of one study indicated that easy-to-understand messages were most persuasive when _____ whereas difficult messages were most persuasive when _____.

    a. audiotaped; written
    b. written; presented live
    c. videotaped; written
    d. videotaped; audiotaped

21. When researchers went to the homes of people from 12 churches shortly the churchgoers had heard sermons opposing racial bigotry, they found that _____ percent spontaneously recalled the sermons.

    a. 10   c. 50
    b. 30   d. 70

22. What effect does distraction have on persuasive communications?

    a. Distraction interferes with reception of the message and as a result the communication is always less persuasive
    b. Distraction facilitates persuasion by inhibiting counterarguing
    c. The results of studies are so conflicting that no one knows
    d. Distraction facilitates persuasion by reducing the sleeper effect

23. People may be more likely to be influenced by peripheral cues such as the appeal of the communicator when they are

    a. image-conscious and thus care less about whether they are right or wrong
    b. highly involved in the issue
    c. analytically inclined
    d. in genuine conflict over the merits of the arguments

24. "Life-cycle" and "generational" explanations both attempt to explain

    a. why the content of messages changes over time
    b. why people have different attitudes depending on their age
    c. why a particular communicator has a different effect on people of different ages
    d. how an emotional appeal builds to a climax in terms of its impact

25. According to the cult researcher Margaret Singer, youths from which class may be most trusting and thus vulnerable to a credible communicator?

    a. lower class   c. upper class
    b. middle class   d. all are equally vulnerable

26. In comparison to people who have a low need for cognition, those who have a high need for cognition

    a. prefer to use simple heuristics (or rules of thumb) in evaluating persuasive appeals
    b. are more susceptible to persuasive attempts that follow the peripheral route
    c. prefer to conserve their mental resources
    d. enjoy thinking and carefully analyzing arguments

27. Social implosion occurs in groups when

    a. ties with people outside the group weaken and each member interacts only with other group members
    b. a cult member overthrows the leader
    c. the poorer members assume leadership and the wealthy become the followers
    d. the cult seeks to attempt major changes in society

28. Attitude inoculation seeks to strengthen beliefs

    a. by giving supporting arguments for the beliefs
    b. by using different channels to communicate the same message
    c. by providing social support for the beliefs
    d. through a weak attack on the beliefs

29. According to the text, the inoculation research suggests that one can build up resistance to persuasion by

    a. listening only to rational appeals
    b. seeking social support for one's beliefs
    c. being an active listener
    d. ignoring emotional appeals

30. College students who live on campus report that they learn most from their contact with

    a. books   c. newspapers and magazines
    b. professors   d. friends and fellow students

31. Which of the following examples shows media influence through a two-step flow of communication?

    a. A teenager buys a shampoo he saw advertised both on television and in a favorite magazine
    b. A gun manufacturer convinces a television station to broadcast a program on the right of citizens to bear arms
    c. A candidate for political office answers questions from a live audience on television
    d. A salesman purchases a new car after talking to a respected friend who read about its advantages in a consumers' magazine

32. Forewarning people that they are going to be exposed to a persuasive communication

    a. distracts them and thus makes them more susceptible to influence
    b. generally has no effect on their susceptibility to influence
    c. elicits fear and reduces their comprehension of the message
    d. makes them more resistant to influence

33. People who are highly involved in an issue will likely be most influenced by the

    a. attractiveness of the source
    b. expertise of the source
    c. strength of the arguments
    d. sheer number of arguments

34. An attractive or a similar communicator would be most effective in changing beliefs about the

    a. health benefits of eating fruits and vegetables
    b. dangers of marijuana use
    c. dangers of driving without wearing seatbelts
    d. advantages of living in a small town versus the country or a large city

35. According to the text, inoculation procedures have been successfully used in helping

    a. motorists to use seat belts
    b. citizens to work for nuclear disarmament
    c. young people to resist peer pressure to smoke
    d. the elderly to resist political pressures to reduce Social Security benefits

36. A gun manufacturer delivers a speech against stricter gun legislation. Because he clearly has a vested interest, his arguments have little initial impact on the audience. However, several weeks later, a survey of the audience indicates that his impact was much greater than first thought. This would be an example of

    a. the recency effect   c. social implosion
    b. the sleeper effect   d. attitude inoculation

37. You have been asked to design an advertising campaign urging people to stop smoking. To be most effective your message should arouse

    a. no fear   c. a low level of fear
    b. a moderate level of fear   d. a high level of fear

38. You have been asked to prepare a speech opposing capital punishment. To be most effective in convincing those who strongly favor the death penalty you should present

    a. a one-sided communication   c. an emotional appeal
    b. a two-sided communication   d. an audiotaped appeal

39. You are one of two candidates being interviewed for a position as superintendent of the city school system. You are notified that one candidate will be interviewed tomorrow evening and the other a week later. The school board will make a decision immediately after the second candidate has been interviewed. If you want the job

    a. you should try to be interviewed first
    b. you should try to be interviewed last
    c. you should try to be interviewed first but only if the school board is composed of college graduates and the other candidate is controversial
    d. you should try to be interviewed first but only if you are more attractive than the other candidate

40. According to research presented in the text, the mass media may be most effective in shaping

    a. one's choice to become a Democrat or Republican
    b. a person's belief in God
    c. one's choice of shampoo to buy
    d. one's attitude toward capital punishment

SHORT ESSAY QUESTIONS

Answer the following questions in the space provided.

1. Briefly describe the two paths to persuasion.

2. List the four major factors psychologists have investigated in research on persuasion.

3. Which factors may influence the perceived credibility of a communicator?

4. Briefly state the research findings regarding each of the following:

   A. fear appeals

   B. message discrepancy

   C. one-sided versus two-sided messages

   D. primacy versus recency effects

5. Contrast the effectiveness of face-to-face personal influence and that of the mass media.

6. Describe how the principles of effective persuasion are implemented in cult indoctrination.

7. Describe what is meant by attitude inoculation.

Chapter Review

1. arguments
   thoughts
   cues
   attractiveness

2. communicator
   how
   audience

3. expert
   trustworthy
   confidently
   self-interest
   talks

4. Attractive
   value
   fact

5. good feelings
   fear

6. discrepancy
   extreme
   moderate
   involved

7. agrees
   unaware

8. primacy
   time
   commitment
   recency

9. experience
   personal
   unfamiliar
   two-step
   opinion

10. moderate
    age

11. thinking
    Forewarning
    counterarguing
    distracting
    persuasion

12. acceptance
    foot-in-the-door

13. charismatic
    emotional
    turning
    isolates

14. commitment
    mild
    counterarguments

Matching Terms

1. c
2. k
3. g
4. a
5. m
6. b
7. n

8. d
9. l
10. e
11. j
12. h
13. f
14. i

True-False Review

1.	T	14.	T
2.	T	15.	F
3.	F	16.	F
4.	F	17.	T
5.	F	18.	T
6.	T	19.	T
7.	T	20.	T
8.	T	21.	F
9.	T	22.	T
10.	T	23.	T
11.	T	24.	F
12.	F	25.	T
13.	F		

Multiple-Choice Practice Test

1.	c	21.	a
2.	d	22.	b
3.	a	23.	a
4.	d	24.	b
5.	d	25.	b
6.	c	26.	d
7.	c	27.	a
8.	c	28.	d
9.	d	29.	c
10.	d	30.	d
11.	b	31.	d
12.	a	32.	d
13.	b	33.	c
14.	c	34.	d
15.	d	35.	c
16.	a	36.	b
17.	d	37.	d
18.	b	38.	b
19.	d	39.	b
20.	c	40.	c

CHAPTER 8

GROUP INFLUENCE

<u>CHAPTER OBJECTIVES</u>

After completing your study of this chapter you should be able to:

1. Define a group.

2. Discuss how we are affected by the presence of other people.

3. Identify the conditions under which social loafing is likely to occur.

4. Describe the psychological state of "deindividuation."

5. Define and explain group polarization.

6. Discuss the causes, symptoms, and prevention of "groupthink."

7. Identify the factors that strengthen minority influence and describe effective leadership.

<u>CHAPTER REVIEW</u>

Supply the words necessary to complete each of the following statements.

WHAT IS A GROUP?
1. A group consists of _____ or more people who, for longer than a few moments, _____ with and influence one another and perceive one another as "us."

SOCIAL FACILITATION
2. The most elementary issue in social psychology concerns how we are affected by the mere _____ of other people. Some early experiments found that one's performance on simple arithmetic and verbal tasks _____

when either observers or co-actors were present. Other experiments found that others'
presence can _____ one's performance.

3. Robert Zajonc reconciled the contradictory findings with a well-known principle from
experimental psychology: Arousal facilitates _____ responses.
Subsequent research indicated that the presence of others boosts performance on
_____ tasks and hinders performance on _____ tasks.

4. Being in a crowd intensifies people's normally _____ or
_____ reactions. In dense situations we may be more responsive to
people's reactions. Crowding also enhances _____.

5. Experiments suggest that we are aroused by others partly as a result of _____
apprehension and partly from a _____ between paying attention to others
and paying attention to the task. Other studies indicate that the presence of others can be
_____ even when the actor is not being evaluated or distracted.

SOCIAL LOAFING

6. Social loafing may occur in work situations where people pool their efforts toward a
_____ goal and where individuals are not _____
for their efforts. Laboratory experiments show that group members work less hard when
performing "_____ tasks." When responsibility is diffused,
individuals may attempt to _____-ride on the group effort.

7. Research indicates that group members loaf less when they are given
_____ objectives, when they are _____ for group
success, and when there is a spirit of _____ to the team.

DEINDIVIDUATION

8. When high levels of social arousal are combined with diffused _____,
people may abandon their normal restraints and lose their sense of _____.
Such "deindividuation" is likely when people feel _____ by
being in a large group or by wearing uniforms.

9. The loss of self-awareness is accompanied by increased responsiveness to the immediate
_____, be it positive or negative. Similarly, circumstances that
increase _____ will decrease deindividuation.

GROUP POLARIZATION

10. James Stoner discovered that group discussion tended to _____ risk-
taking. In seeking to explain the "risky shift," investigators discovered that discussion
tends to _____ whatever is the initially dominant point of view.

11. Informational and normative influence explain why groups intensify _____.
Group discussion elicits a pooling of persuasive _____ that favor

124

the dominant point of view. In addition, social _____ with others reveals surprising support for one's initial inclination. To be perceived favorably, a person expresses stronger opinions.

GROUPTHINK

12. A group's desire for _____ can override its realistic appraisal of alternative courses of action. Irving Janis suggested that groupthink is most likely to occur when the group is cohesive, is _____ from contrary viewpoints, and has a_____ leader.

13. The symptoms of groupthink include (1) an _____ of invulnerability, (2) rationalization, (3) unquestioned belief in the group's _____, (4) _____ views of the opposition, (5) pressure to conform, (6) _____ of misgivings, (7) an illusion of unanimity, and (8) "_____," who protect the group from unpleasant information.

THE INFLUENCE OF THE MINORITY

14. Research indicates that a minority is most influential when it is _____ and persistent in its views, when its actions convey an image of _____, and when it elicits some defections from the majority. Even if it fails to persuade the majority to adopt its position, the minority may increase the majority's _____ and willingness to consider other alternatives. One example of the power of individuals is _____, the process by which certain group members motivate and guide the group. Research indicates that effective supervisors score high on tests of both _____ and _____ leadership.

MATCHING TERMS

Write the letter of the term on the right before the appropriate number on the left.

_____ 1. Occurs on additive tasks.	a. social comparison
_____ 2. Enhances a minority's influence.	b. deindividuation
_____ 3. People who benefit from the group but give little in return.	c. free riders
_____ 4. Discovered the risky shift.	d. social facilitation
_____ 5. A way of evaluating one's opinions and abilities.	e. social loafing
_____ 6. The best supported explanation for group polarization.	f. evaluation apprehension
_____ 7. Studied minority influence.	g. risky shift
_____ 8. Was revised in favor of group polarization.	h. self-censorship
_____ 9. Occurs in groups that foster anonymity.	i. self-confidence
_____ 10. Studied groupthink.	j. informational influence
_____ 11. The strengthening of dominant responses due to the presence of others.	k. Janis
_____ 12. Partially explains why the presence of others arouses us.	l. pluralistic ignorance
_____ 13. A false impression of how others are thinking or feeling.	m. Stoner
_____ 14. A symptom of groupthink.	n. Moscovici

Circle T if the statement is true and F if it is false.

T F 1. Social psychologists define a group as any collection of two or more individuals.

T F 2. Co-actors are people engaged in some competitive activity.

T F 3. The presence of other people facilitates the performance of easy tasks and hinders performance of difficult tasks.

T F 4. The social-facilitation effect has been explained in terms of informational influence.

T F 5. The *minority slowness effect* refers to the tendency for people with minority views to express them less quickly than do people in the majority

T F 6. Researchers agree that all great leaders share common traits.

T F 7. Whenever people are in a crowd, they experience discomfort and stress.

T F 8. Some research indicates that effective supervisors score high on tests of both task and social leadership.

T F 9. Social loafing is not likely to occur in athletic contests in which one person competes against another.

T F 10. Social loafing seems to occur because of poor coordination of individual efforts within a group.

T F 11. Expecting to interact with someone again serves to increase effort on team projects.

T F 12. Social loafing decreases when the size of a group increases.

T F 13. Anonymity inevitably has a negative impact on group members.

T F 14. Research indicates that group discussion invariably increases risk taking.

T F 15. Studies of social loafing grew out of earlier research on the risky shift.

T F 16. *Group polarization* refers to a split within a group.

T F 17. *Pluralistic ignorance* refers to a false impression of what most other people are thinking, feeling, or responding.

T F 18. The concept of groupthink grew out of an analysis of poor decisions made in business and industry.

T F 19. Transformational leadership motivates people to identify with, and commit themselves to, the group's mission.

T F 20. Groups of eyewitnesses give accounts of a crime that are much more accurate than those provided by isolated individuals.

T F 21. Brainstorming face to face with other people generates more creative ideas than does brainstorming all alone.

T F 22. One prescription for preventing groupthink is to have one or more members assigned the role of devil's advocate.

T F 23. Two weather forecasters working together will come up with a more accurate forecast than either of them will come up with working alone.

T F 24. Some psychologists believe that groupthink symptoms may have characterized the decision to start the Iraq War.

T F 25. Researchers have found that a minority person who defected from the majority was more persuasive than one who consistently voiced the minority position.

MULTIPLE-CHOICE PRACTICE TEST

Circle the correct letter.

1. Which form of social influence discussed in Chapter 8 does not necessarily involve an interacting group?

   a. group polarization
   b. groupthink
   c. minority influence
   d. social facilitation

2. The definition of a group given in the text and provided by Marvin Shaw states that a group consists of

   a. any collection of individuals
   b. two or more people who interact and influence one another
   c. two or more people who share similar values
   d. a cohesive collection of individuals

3. Which of the following is true?

   a. Others' presence improves the accuracy with which people keep a metal stick in contact with a disk on a moving turntable
   b. Ants excavate less sand in the presence of other ants
   c. In the presence of others, students take more time to learn a simple maze and less time to learn one that is complex
   d. Joggers run more slowly when jogging with someone else than when jogging alone

4. Early experiments found that the presence of others improved people's efficiency at

   a. learning nonsense syllables
   b. crossing out designated letters
   c. performing complex multiplication problems
   d. learning foreign language words

5. James Michaels and his colleagues found that in the presence of observers,

   a. good pool players shot better and poor pool players shot worse
   b. students playing checkers and chess played worse
   c. good pool players shot worse and poor pool players shot better
   d. students playing checkers played better and students playing chess played worse

6. Studies of athletic performance have shown that

   a. in soccer, home teams win only half their games
   b. the drives of professional golfers are shorter when an audience is present
   c. if self-conscious basketball players analyze their body movements while shooting critical free throws, they are more likely to make them
   d. in college and professional sports, home teams win about 6 in 10 games

7. Research indicates that crowding hampers performance on _____ tasks.

   a. verbal   c. simple
   b. motor   d. difficult

8. Research indicates that people perform best when their co-actor is

   a. not watching them   c. of the opposite sex
   b. slightly superior   d. highly competitive

9. Social facilitation and social loafing have been explained in terms of difference in

   a. evaluation concern   c. cognitive dissonance
   b. informational influence   d. group polarization

10. Which process helps explain both social loafing and deindividuation?

    a. self-censorship
    b. minority influence
    c. diffusion of responsibility
    d. group polarization

11. Research indicates that being in a crowd _____ positive reactions and _____ negative reactions.

    a. intensifies; intensifies
    b. weakens; intensifies
    c. intensifies; weakens
    d. weakens; weakens

12. Which of the following is false?

    a. Groups of friends loaf less than groups of strangers
    b. Israel's communal kibbutz farms have outproduced Israel's noncollective farms
    c. Research completed in Japan, Thailand, and India indicates that social loafing does not occur in less individualistic, more group-centered cultures
    d. Students pumped exercise bikes more energetically when they knew they were being individually monitored than when they thought their output was being pooled with that of other riders

13. Experiments show that people in groups loaf less when

    a. the task is challenging
    b. they are in an unfamiliar setting
    c. they have a strong sense of external control
    d. the task is routine

14. Women dressed in Ku Klux Klan-style coats and hoods were more aggressive than those who were visible and wearing name tags. This finding is best explained in terms of the process of

    a. groupthink
    b. deindividuation
    c. reactance
    d. social facilitation

15. The research on deindividuation shows that a group experience that diminishes people's self-consciousness also tends to

    a. decrease their emotional arousal
    b. decrease their normal inhibitions
    c. increase their feelings of self-esteem
    d. increase their sensitivity to their own conscience

16. The term *risky shift* was used to refer to the finding of

    a. groups being riskier than individuals
    b. individuals being riskier than groups
    c. males being riskier than females
    d. people becoming less risky as they grow older

17. Studies of the risky shift eventually led to formulation of

    a. social comparison theory
    b. the group polarization hypothesis
    c. the social facilitation effect
    d. the social-loafing effect

18. Group polarization is most likely to occur in a group

    a. of like-minded people
    b. of unintelligent people
    c. of persons with differing value systems
    d. discussing political issues

19. Myers and Bishop set up groups of relatively prejudiced and unprejudiced high school students and asked them to respond both before and after discussion to issues involving racial attitudes. Results indicated that after discussion

    a. both groups were more prejudiced
    b. both groups were less prejudiced
    c. the individuals who were relatively unprejudiced became even less prejudiced and the individuals who were relatively prejudiced became even more prejudiced
    d. the individuals who were relatively unprejudiced became more prejudiced and the individuals who were relatively prejudiced became less prejudiced

20. Leaders who motivate others to identify with and commit themselves to the group's mission are known as _____ leaders.

    a. social
    b. transformational
    c. executive
    d. directive

21. According to Janis, which of the following was the product of groupthink?

    a. the Truman administration's formulation of the Marshall Plan after World War II
    b. the Truman administration's decision to drop the atomic bomb on Hiroshima
    c. the Johnson administration's decision to escalate the Vietnam War
    d. the Nixon administration's decision to freeze prices

22. An analysis of terrorist organizations around the world suggests that the extremist activities of these groups may be understood in terms of the process of

    a. social loafing
    b. social facilitation
    c. minority influence
    d. group polarization

23. According to the text, weather forecasting, game shows, and Google all demonstrate

    a. the danger of groupthink
    b. transformational leadership
    c. the wisdom of crowds
    d. group polarization

24. Patrick Laughlin reported that if only two members of a six-person group are initially correct in solving an analogy problem, they

    a. rarely convince the others
    b. convince the others one-third of the time
    c. convince the others two-thirds of the time
    d. always convince the others

25. The text suggests that the hostile flaming that sometimes occurs on the Internet is fostered by

    a. responsibility diffusion
    b. anonymity
    c. social norming
    d. the minority slowness effect

26. Research suggests that minorities are less persuasive regarding _____ than regarding _____.

    a. fact; attitude
    b. attitude; fact
    c. principle; practice
    d. practice; principle

27. Which of the following is not a symptom of groupthink?

    a. unquestioned belief in the group's morality
    b. rationalization
    c. conformity pressure
    d. social loafing

28. Moscovici and his associates found that if a minority judges blue slides to be green,

    a. this fact has no effect on the judgments of the majority
    b. members of the majority will occasionally agree but only if the minority is consistent
    c. members of the majority demonstrate reactance by judging green slides to be blue
    d. female but not male members of the majority will occasionally agree

29. Groupthink occurs when group members desire

    a. control   c. power
    b. harmony   d. freedom

30. Research indicates that a minority member who _____ is persuasive.

    a. wavers
    b. has defected from the majority
    c. tends to be introverted
    d. appears impatient

31. Studies done in India, Taiwan, and Iran found that the most effective supervisors in coal mines, banks, and government offices scored

    a. high on both task and social leadership
    b. high on task and low on social leadership
    c. high on either task or social leadership but not high on both
    d. low on task and high on social leadership

32. Tom, a successful foreman in a large furniture factory, emphasizes the attainment of production goals and sets high standards for the workers under him. Tom's style is an example of _____ leadership.

    a. normative   c. autocratic
    b. task   d. Type A

33. The presence of others would most likely improve performance on

    a. raking up leaves
    b. solving crossword puzzles
    c. learning foreign language words
    d. solving complex mathematical puzzles

34. Who of the following would be considered co-actors?

    a. four people doing push-ups in an exercise class
    b. two people playing bridge
    c. eight competitors running a 5-kilometer race
    d. two children playing badminton

35. After an exciting soccer game in which the home team loses, a crowd of fans throws garbage and begins to tear up the field. This behavior is best understood in terms of

    a. group polarization   c. groupthink
    b. deindividuation   d. social facilitation

36. Which of the following is least likely to be considered a group as defined in the text?

    a. a husband and wife talking over dinner
    b. a committee of eight discussing the problem of neighborhood crime
    c. four seven-year-olds playing hide-and-go-seek
    d. seven people waiting at a bus stop

37. The presence of others would least likely improve performance in

    a. playing chess   c. running
    b. weightlifting   d. the broad jump

38. Social loafing would least likely occur

    a. in a boys' club trying to raise money by holding a Saturday car wash
    b. in a relay race in which each team member's performance is timed
    c. in a community garden where each family is expected to contribute whatever free time they have
    d. in a work crew building a new highway

39. Individuals who tend to favor stiff penalties for drunk drivers come together to discuss various ways of dealing with the problem of intoxicated drivers. The group polarization hypothesis predicts that after group discussion,

    a. the individuals will favor even more severe penalties for drunk drivers
    b. the individuals will tend to become more tolerant of drunk drivers
    c. the individuals will be divided into two groups opposed over the best way to deal with drunk drivers
    d. the individuals will favor a rehabilitation program rather than a jail sentence for drunk drivers

40. Which of the following is a comment you are least likely to hear made within a group characterized by groupthink?

    a. "Our critics are not very smart."
    b. "Our past decisions have always been right."
    c. "Let's make the decision and get out of here. I've got more important things to do."
    d. "It seems to me we are all in agreement on this, so let's proceed."

SHORT ESSAY QUESTIONS

Answer the following questions in the space provided.

1. Define *group*.

2. Explain how the meaning of the term *social facilitation* has changed.

3. Explain what is meant by the term *free riders*. When is free riding most likely to occur?

4. What is *deindividuation*? Briefly describe its causes and effects.

5. Provide two explanations for group polarization.

6. List the major symptoms of groupthink.

7. Identify two factors that contribute to the effectiveness of minority influence.

ANSWER KEY

Chapter Review

1. two
   interact

2. presence
   improved
   hinder

3. dominant
   easy
   difficult

4. positive
   negative
   arousal

5. evaluation
   conflict
   arousing

6. common
   accountable
   additive
   free

7. challenging
   rewarded
   commitment

8. responsibility
   individuality
   anonymity

9. situation
   self-awareness

10. increase
    enhance

11. opinions
    arguments
    comparison

12. harmony
    isolated
    directive

13. illusion
    morality
    stereotyped
    self-censorship
    mindguards

14. consistent
    self-confidence
    self-doubts
    leadership
    task
    social

Matching Terms

1. e
2. i
3. c
4. m
5. a
6. j
7. n

8. g
9. b
10. k
11. d
12. f
13. l
14. h

True-False Review

1.	F	14.	F
2.	F	15.	F
3.	T	16.	F
4.	F	17.	T
5.	T	18.	F
6.	F	19.	T
7.	F	20.	T
8.	T	21.	F
9.	T	22.	T
10.	F	23.	T
11.	T	24.	T
12.	F	25.	T
13.	F		

Multiple-Choice Practice Test

1.	d	21.	c
2.	b	22.	d
3.	a	23.	c
4.	b	24.	c
5.	a	25.	b
6.	d	26.	a
7.	d	27.	d
8.	b	28.	b
9.	a	29.	b
10.	c	30.	b
11.	a	31.	a
12.	c	32.	b
13.	a	33.	a
14.	b	34.	a
15.	b	35.	b
16.	a	36.	d
17.	b	37.	a
18.	a	38.	b
19.	c	39.	a
20.	b	40.	c

CHAPTER 9

PREJUDICE

CHAPTER OBJECTIVES

After completing your study of this chapter you should be able to:

1. Distinguish between prejudice and discrimination.

2. Trace recent trends in racial and gender prejudice in the United States.

3. Explain how unequal status and the socialization process may fuel prejudice.

4. Demonstrate how prejudice is maintained through conformity and institutional supports.

5. Explain the scapegoat theory of prejudice and discuss the human motives that foster ingroup favoritism.

6. Show how stereotypes and prejudiced attitudes can be a by-product of our normal thinking processes.

7. Describe the just world phenomenon.

8. Explain how stereotypes tend to perpetuate themselves and resist change.

CHAPTER REVIEW

Supply the words necessary to complete each of the following statements.

WHAT IS THE NATURE AND POWER OF PREJUDICE?

1. Prejudice is a preconceived negative _____ of a group and its individual members. The beliefs supporting prejudice are called _____, and they are often inaccurate and resistant to new information.

2. Discrimination is unjustified negative _____ toward a group or its members. The terms *racism* and _____ refer to institutional practices that discriminate, even when there is no prejudicial intent. Prejudice has overt _____ components and subtle _____ components.

3. Survey research suggests that racial prejudice in the United States has _____ since the early 1940s. Although less blatant, prejudice exists in _____ forms and is also evident from experiments that have assessed people's actual _____ toward Blacks and Whites. Prejudiced attitudes and discriminatory behavior surface when they can hide behind the screen of some other _____.

4. While strong _____ stereotypes still exist, prejudice against women has _____. For example, people no longer _____ women's work. However, as is true of racial prejudice, _____ gender prejudice still lives. Around the world, people tend to prefer having baby _____.

WHAT ARE THE SOCIAL SOURCES OF PREJUDICE?

5. _____ status breeds prejudice as the group that enjoys superiority seeks to justify its standing. Those high in social _____ orientation try to maintain high status more than do others. The _____ personality demonstrates intolerance for weakness and a submissive _____ for ingroup authorities.

6. _____ is sometimes used to justify injustice and may explain why American church members are _____ racially prejudiced than nonmembers. However, faithful church attenders are _____ prejudiced than occasional attenders and the devout are _____ prejudiced than the nominally religious.

7. Once prejudice becomes a social norm, it is maintained partly through the inertia of _____. In addition, _____ supports, for example, government, _____, and the media can serve to bolster widespread prejudice.

WHAT ARE THE MOTIVATIONAL SOURCES OF PREJUDICE?

8. _____ often evokes hostility, which may be vented on scapegoats. This phenomenon of "_____ aggression" may have contributed to the lynching of African Americans in the South after the Civil War. An important source of frustration is _____: one group's goal fulfillment becomes the other group's frustration.

9. People are also motivated to view themselves and their groups as _____ to other groups. The mere experience of being formed into groups may promote _____ bias. When the need to _____ is met, people become more

accepting of outgroups.   The motivation to avoid _____ can lead people to modify their thoughts and actions.

WHAT ARE THE COGNITIVE SOURCES OF PREJUDICE?

10. Stereotyped beliefs are also by-products of our normal _____ processes. Once people are categorized into groups, we are likely to exaggerate the _____ within groups and the _____ between them. In viewing another group, we also tend to perceive that its members "act and look alike, we don't."

11. _____ people draw our attention making us aware of differences we otherwise do not notice. We also better remember vivid cases and may use them to judge an entire _____.   Our attentiveness to unusual occurrences can also create _____ correlations. For example, a minority person committing an unusual crime may lead us to associate such people with such behavior.

12. _____ errors can bias people's explanations of group members' behaviors. By way of _____-_____ bias we explain away outgroup members' positive behaviors and attribute their negative behaviors to their dispositions. Blaming victims also results from believing the world is a _____ place in which people get what they deserve.

WHAT ARE THE CONSEQUENCES OF PREJUDICE?

13. Stereotypes can be self-_____. Their existence can prevent their _____. Stereotype _____ is a self-confirming apprehension that one will be evaluated based on a negative stereotype.   When people get to know a person, they may set aside their stereotypes. Stereotypes are more potent when people judge _____ individuals and when they are deciding policies that affect entire groups. Stereotypes can subtly color our assessments of individuals' behaviors. For example, we evaluate people more extremely when their behavior _____ our stereotypes.

141

MATCHING TERMS

Write the letter of the term on the right before the appropriate number on the left.

_____ 1. Belief in the superiority of one's ethnic or cultural group.

a. outgroup homogeneity effect

_____ 2. Individuals' prejudicial attitudes and discriminatory behavior toward people of a given sex.

b. realistic group conflict theory

c. authoritarianism

_____ 3. Unjustified negative behavior toward a group or its members.

d. scapegoat theory

_____ 4. Explaining away outgroup members' positive behaviors while attributing negative behaviors to the members' dispositions.

e. ethnocentrism

f. subgrouping

_____ 5. Institutional practices that subordinate people of a given race.

g. stereotype threat

_____ 6. Tending toward punitiveness in thinking.

h. prejudice

_____ 7. A preconceived negative judgment of a group and its members.

i. discrimination

j. racism

_____ 8. Forming a new stereotype of "professional, middle-class Blacks."

k. stereotype

_____ 9. People deserve what they get.

l. sexism

_____ 10. An explanation for the lynchings of African-Americans in the South.

m. group-serving bias

n. the just world phenomenon

_____ 11. A belief about the personal attributes of a group of people.

_____ 12. Concern that one will be evaluated based on a negative stereotype.

_____ 13. Prejudice arises when groups compete for scarce resources.

_____ 14. Perceiving outgroup members as more similar to one another than are ingroup members.

TRUE-FALSE REVIEW

Circle T if the statement is true and F if it is false.

T F   1. Prejudice is unjustified negative behavior toward a group and its members.

T F   2. Weight discrimination is notably greater than race or gender discrimination.

T F   3. The persistence and omnipresence of gender stereotypes lead some evolutionary psychologists to believe they reflect innate, stable reality.

T F   4. Racism refers not only to attitudes but also to behavior and institutional practices that subordinate people of a given race.

T F   5. Prejudiced and stereotypic evaluations can occur outside people's awareness.

T F   6. People everywhere perceive women as more agreeable and men as more outgoing.

T F   7. Sorority sisters perceive the members of any other sorority as more diverse than their own.

T F   8. Strong gender stereotypes exist and members of the stereotyped group accept the stereotypes.

T F   9. Those high in social dominance orientation tend to view people in terms of hierarchies.

T F 10. Half of African Americans perceive themselves as having faced discrimination within the last 30 days.

T F 11. Those for whom religion is an end in itself express less prejudice than those for whom religion is a means to an end.

T F 12. Some research indicates that composing groups X and Y with only a flip of the coin is sufficient to produce ingroup bias.

T F 13. Children of employed women have less stereotyped views of men and women.

T F 14. Ingroup bias results as much or more from perceiving that one's own group is good as from a sense that other groups are bad.

T F 15. Compared to nonprejudiced people, prejudiced people take less time to categorize others by race.

T F 16. The authoritarian personality is prejudiced against Blacks but not against other minority groups.

143

T F 17. When White and Black students are shown faces of a few White and Black individuals and then asked to pick these individuals out of a photographic lineup, both White and Black students more accurately recognize the White faces than the Black.

T F 18. We are more prone to ingroup bias when our group is large and higher in status relative to an outgroup.

T F 19. Teachers' stereotypes of motivational and achievement differences in students from different gender, ethnic, and class backgrounds have little basis in reality.

T F 20. Hate crimes have fluctuated with unemployment in recent decades.

T F 21. Different brain regions are involved in automatic and consciously controlled stereotyping.

T F 22. People often evaluate individuals more positively than the groups the individuals compose.

T F 23. The need to believe in a just world provides an explanation for why we disparage victims of injustice.

T F 24. Research indicates that people's judgments of a person's work are unaffected by whether the work is attributed to a man or to a woman.

T F 25. As African American students move from 8th to 10th grade, there is a weakening connection between their school performance and their self-esteem.

MULTIPLE-CHOICE PRACTICE TEST

Circle the correct letter.

1. Prejudice is a negative _____ whereas discrimination is negative
    _____.

    a. belief; feeling   c. attitude; behavior
    b. generalization; practice   d. stereotype; practice

2. Stereotypes are to discrimination as _____ are to
    _____.

    a. categories; feelings   c. emotions; practice
    b. attitudes; actions   d. beliefs; behavior

3. Racism
   a. can refer to institutional practices that discriminate even when there is no prejudicial intent
   b. refers to institutional practices that discriminate but only if there is prejudicial intent
   c. refers only to individuals' prejudicial attitudes
   d. refers only to individuals' discriminatory behavior

4. Survey research on racial prejudice in the United States indicates that

   a. racial prejudice has increased since the 1980s
   b. racial prejudice increased from the 1950s to 1970s but has decreased since then
   c. racial prejudice has decreased since the 1940s
   d. the level of racial prejudice has remained unchanged since 1952

5. When Steven Spencer and his colleagues gave a very difficult math test to men and women students and told them that there were no gender differences on the test, the women

   a. outperformed the men
   b. performed as well as the men
   c. performed more poorly than the men
   d. with more liberal attitudes outperformed the women with more conservative attitudes

6. Which of the following is true?

   a. Strong gender stereotypes continue to exist
   b. Prejudice against women has not declined in the last 20 years
   c. Racial stereotypes are stronger than gender stereotypes
   d. Stereotypes are the same as prejudices

7. Most Americans agree that

   a. the activities of married women are best confined to the home and family
   b. they would probably move if Black people came to live in great numbers in their neighborhood
   c. the two sexes are equally emotional
   d. they would vote for a qualified woman whom their party nominated for president

8. People who are high in social dominance orientation tend to oppose policies such as

   a. affirmative action
   b. the death penalty for homicide
   c. tax cuts for the well off
   d. increased spending for national defense

9. In the 1950s, racial integration was accepted in Indiana steel mills and West Virginia coal mines. However, in the neighborhoods of those employed in the mills and mines, segregation was practiced. This is an example of how prejudice may be based in

   a. authoritarianism   c. frustration
   b. the just world phenomenon   d. conformity

10. Automatic stereotyping is to _____ as consciously controlled stereotyping is to

    _____

    a. the left cerebral hemisphere; the right cerebral hemisphere
    b. males; females
    c. the amygdala; the frontal cortex
    d. discrimination; prejudice

11. Which best summarizes the research findings on people's evaluations of work attributed to women or to men?

    a. People's judgments of someone's work are not significantly affected by whether the work is attributed to a male or a female
    b. Both males and females show a tendency to deprecate women's work
    c. Males show a tendency to deprecate women's work whereas females' judgments are not affected by whether the work is attributed to a male or a female
    d. Females but not males show a tendency to deprecate women's work

12. Social psychologists' most recent explanation of prejudice emphasizes _____ sources.

    a. social   c. emotional
    b. cognitive   d. political

13. The tendency of lynchings to increase in years when cotton prices were low was cited in the text as evidence for

    a. the just world phenomenon
    b. the ultimate attribution error
    c. the scapegoat theory
    d. psychoanalytic theory

14. Realistic group conflict theory suggests that prejudice arises

    a. where there is a long history of distrust between two groups
    b. when a new group moves into an area
    c. when groups fail to communicate clearly with one another
    d. when groups compete for scarce resources

15. The fact that we may retain from childhood a habitual automatic dislike of people for whom we now express respect illustrates

    a. Gause's law
    b. the dual attitude system
    c. social dominance orientation
    d. the split brain phenomenon

16. Studies by Pettigrew of Whites in South Africa and the American South revealed that during the 1950s

    a. prejudice had its basis in competition for housing and jobs
    b. those who were prejudiced were authoritarian personalities
    c. prejudice was based in displaced aggression
    d. those who conformed most to other social norms were also the most prejudiced

17. The idea that we find it useful to put people, ourselves included, into categories is an important assumption of _____ theory.

    a. just world   c. social identity
    b. realistic group conflict   d. cognitive bias

18. Which of the following characteristics is particularly applicable to the authoritarian personality?

    a. being intolerant of weakness
    b. experiencing a happy childhood
    c. occupying a political office with considerable authority
    d. being an only child

19. Bob Altemeyer reports that people high in _____ and high in
    _____ are among the most prejudiced in society.

    a. social dominance orientation; authoritarian personality
    b. self-serving bias; need to belong
    c. group-serving bias; conformity
    d. just world thinking; self-esteem

20. In experiments in which some people are made to appear overweight, they are perceived as

    a. happier   c. more sociable
    b. less intelligent   d. less emotional

21. Gallup poll reports indicate that the average American tends to _____ the U.S. Black and Hispanic populations and to _____ the percentage of gay men and lesbian women.

   a. underestimate; underestimate
   b. overestimate; underestimate
   c. underestimate; overestimate
   d. overestimate; overestimate

22. The group-serving bias seems to be relatively uncharacteristic of groups that stress

   a. individualism   c. modesty
   b. honesty   d. intelligence

23. Reminding people of their death intensifies

   a. ingroup favoritism   c. stigma consciousness
   b. stereotype threat   d. the women-are-wonderful effect

24. According to the text, the authoritarian personality is an example of

   a. how conformity supports prejudice
   b. a cognitive source of prejudice
   c. how socialization can contribute to prejudice
   d. how social inequalities can breed prejudice

25. The co-occurrence of two distinctive events can create

   a. belief in a just world   c. illusion of control
   b. illusory correlation   d. the ultimate attribution error

26. Students were told the actions of 50 men, 10 of whom had performed either nonviolent crimes or violent crimes. When later asked to make judgments about the men,

   a. the subjects shown the list with the violent crimes most overestimated the number of criminal acts
   b. the subjects shown the list with the nonviolent crimes most overestimated the number of criminal acts
   c. the subjects judged all the men to be members of outgroups
   d. male subjects made more accurate judgments about the number of criminal acts than did female subjects

27. In one study, students were told that various members of "Group A" or "Group B" did either something desirable or something undesirable. While many more statements described members of Group A than Group B, both groups were associated with nine desirable behaviors for every four undesirable behaviors. Results indicated

    a. that students perceived members of Group B more negatively
    b. that students perceived members of Group A more negatively
    c. no differences in the students' perceptions of the groups
    d. that authoritarian students viewed Group A more negatively

28. Researchers who used a uniform strategy to negotiate the lowest price on a new car found that _____ were offered the highest, or worst, price.

    a. White males   c. White females
    b. Black males   d. Black females

29. A study of photographs in magazines and newspapers revealed that prominence was given to

    a. men's faces and women's bodies
    b. men's bodies and women's faces
    c. Whites' faces and Blacks' bodies
    d. Whites' bodies and Blacks' faces

30. John Williams and his colleagues found that people everywhere perceive women as more _____ and men as more _____.

    a. outgoing; reserved
    b. agreeable; outgoing
    c. depressed; contented
    d. talkative; disagreeable

31. According to Lerner, our need to believe in a just world often leads us to blame

    a. fate   c. the social structure
    b. supernatural forces   d. the victim

32. According to the text, stereotypes are resistant to change because

    a. for the most part, they are accurate reflections of reality
    b. our prejudgments influence how we interpret and process information
    c. they are always based on an authoritarian attitude that is blind to disconfirming evidence
    d. they are held by people with low intelligence

33. Mr. Watson's belief that Blacks are lazy is an example of _____.
His refusal to rent an apartment to a Black family is an example of _____.

   a. a stereotype; sexism
   b. discrimination; prejudice
   c. a stereotype; discrimination
   d. racism; prejudice

34. Forming a new stereotype of "serious, college-bound young people" who deviate from one's negative stereotype of irresponsible teenagers is an example of

   a. just world thinking
   b. authoritarianism
   c. subgrouping
   d. external attribution

35. Which of the following would you <u>not</u> expect to be true of the authoritarian personality?

   a. discriminating against American Indians
   b. wanting to achieve high social status
   c. being respectful of police
   d. being opposed to capital punishment

36. Which of the following statements would be an example of group-serving bias?

   a. Veryl believes that women are unemployed because of discrimination and that men are unemployed because of low motivation
   b. Sue believes that members of her own family are prejudiced and that her husband's family is tolerant
   c. Chuck believes that mistakes made by both men and women are due to low intelligence
   d. Bill believes that groups outperform individuals in solving problems

37. The just world phenomenon may lead us to believe that an unemployed person is

   a. a victim of discrimination
   b. lazy
   c. in need of sympathy
   d. in need of a retraining program

38. John has just failed a chemistry test. He goes back to his apartment and criticizes his roommate's choice of music. What term best describes John's behavior?

   a. institutionalized aggression
   b. just world action
   c. displaced aggression
   d. authoritarian regression

39. Which of the following cases is an example of racism as the term is defined in the text?

   a. Mr. Jones' refusal to rent his apartments to Chinese
   b. Mrs. Smith's prejudice toward Hispanics
   c. a government regulation that prevents inner-city residents from being recruited to serve as Army officers
   d. all of the above

40. The results of one social-psychological study indicated that observers who discovered that a fellow worker had received a large prize as the result of a random drawing subsequently concluded that he had in fact worked especially hard. This is an example of

   a. vivid, anecdotal information being more important than base-rate data
   b. disguised hostility
   c. outgroup bias
   d. just world phenomenon

SHORT ESSAY QUESTIONS

Answer the following questions in the space provided.

1. Distinguish among prejudice, discrimination, and racism.

2. What evidence indicates that racial prejudice still exists in the United States?

3. What evidence suggests that gender prejudice is declining?

4. Explain how unequal status breeds prejudice.

5. Describe two institutional supports for prejudice.

6. Discuss the scapegoat theory of prejudice.

7. Describe two ways in which our normal thinking processes can be a source of prejudice.

8. Describe the just world phenomenon.

9. Explain the concept of stereotype threat.

ANSWER KEY

Chapter Review

1. judgment
   stereotypes

2. behavior
   sexism
   conscious
   automatic

3. declined
   subtle
   behavior
   motive

4. gender
   declined
   deprecate
   subtle
   boys

5. Unequal
   dominance
   authoritarian
   respect

6. Religion
   more
   less
   less

7. conformity
   institutional
   schools

8. Frustration
   displaced
   competition

9. superior
   ingroup
   belong
   prejudice

10. thinking
    similarities
    differences

11. Distinctive
    group
    illusory

12. Attribution
    group-serving
    just

13. perpetuating
    change
    threat
    unknown
    violates

Matching Terms

1.	e	8.	f
2.	l	9.	n
3.	i	10.	d
4.	m	11.	k
5.	j	12.	g
6.	c	13.	b
7.	h	14.	a

True-False Review

1.	F	14.	T
2.	T	15.	F
3.	T	16.	F
4.	T	17.	F
5.	T	18.	F
6.	T	19.	F
7.	F	20.	F
8.	T	21.	T
9.	T	22.	T
10.	T	23.	T
11.	T	24.	T
12.	T	25.	T
13.	T		

Multiple-Choice Practice Test

1. c	21. d
2. d	22. c
3. a	23. a
4. c	24. c
5. b	25. b
6. a	26. a
7. d	27. a
8. a	28. d
9. d	29. a
10. c	30. b
11. a	31. d
12. b	32. b
13. c	33. c
14. d	34. c
15. b	35. d
16. d	36. a
17. c	37. b
18. a	38. c
19. a	39. d
20. b	40. d

CHAPTER 10

AGGRESSION

After completing your study of this chapter you should be able to:

1. Define *aggression* and explain the difference between hostile aggression and instrumental aggression.

2. Discuss the instinct view of aggression.

3. Describe biological influences on aggression.

4. Identify the causes and consequences of frustration.

5. Discuss the social learning view of aggression.

6. Identify aversive experiences that tend to provoke aggression.

7. Describe the impact of the media on thinking and behavior.

8. Discuss ways of reducing aggression.

CHAPTER REVIEW

Supply the words necessary to complete each of the following statements.

WHAT IS AGGRESSION?

1. Aggression is physical or verbal behavior intended to cause _____.

   _____ aggression springs from anger and aims to injure.

   _____ aggression also aims to injure but only as a means to some

   other end.

WHAT ARE SOME THEORIES OF AGGRESSION?

2. Sigmund Freud and Konrad Lorenz argued that aggression is _____. They maintained that if aggressive energy is not discharged it builds until it _____. Evolutionary psychologists suggest that the _____ value of aggression helps explain the high level of male-male aggression across history.

3. Although the evidence does not support the instinct view, research has identified _____ influences upon aggression including _____ systems, heredity, and blood _____.

4. A second theory, proposed by John Dollard and his associates in 1939, is that _____, or the blocking of goal-directed behavior, invariably leads to aggression. Leonard Berkowitz, in a revision of the theory, states that frustration produces _____, an emotional readiness to aggress. A frustrated person is especially likely to lash out when aggressive _____ pull the cork.

5. Frustration is created by a gap between our _____ and our attainments. _____ deprivation is the perception that we are less well off than others to whom we compare ourselves.

6. _____ learning theory presents aggression as learned behavior. Through experience and by _____ others' success we learn that aggression often pays. Albert Bandura contends that aggressive acts are most likely when we are _____ by aversive experiences and it seems safe and _____ to aggress.

WHAT ARE SOME INFLUENCES ON AGGRESSION?

7. Animals' reactions to shock indicate that _____ may provoke aggressive acts. Temporary climate variations affect one's behavior, and _____ has been shown to increase aggression. Being _____ by another is also conducive to aggression.

8. Research indicates that our experience of emotion depends on how we _____ our bodily states. Thus arousal from almost any source, even physical _____ or sexual stimulation, can be interpreted as _____ and lead to aggression. Studies indicate that viewing pornography distorts _____ of sexual reality and may contribute to men's _____ toward women. Rather than advocate censorship, many psychologists favor "_____ _____ training."

9. The _____ hypothesis suggests that viewing violent drama enables people to release pent-up hostility. Research indicates that viewing violence produces an _____ in aggressive behavior especially in people who are provoked.

It seems to _____ viewers to aggression and to alter their
_____ of reality. Recent research indicates that video
_____ are teaching tools that can also promote violence.

10. Circumstances that provoke individuals to aggress can provoke
_____ to do likewise. In fact, social interaction can actually
_____ the aggressive reactions of individuals.

HOW CAN AGGRESSION BE REDUCED?

11. The catharsis hypothesis, which predicts that the aggressive drive will be _____
after one releases aggressive energy, has not been confirmed. In some studies aggressing
has actually led to _____ aggression.

12. Social learning theory proposes we reduce aggression by reducing _____
stimulation and by _____ and modeling cooperative,
nonaggressive behavior. _____ is considerably less effective
because it provides aversive stimulation and models the very behavior it seeks to prevent.

13. Since aggression is increased in the presence of aggressive cues, limiting the availability
of _____ can reduce violence.

MATCHING TERMS

Write the letter of the term on the right before the appropriate number on the left.

_____	1. Redirecting aggression to a safer target.	a. hostile aggression
_____	2. The blocking of goal-directed behavior.	b. prosocial behavior
_____	3. Innate, unlearned behavior exhibited by all members of a species.	c. relative deprivation
_____	4. An author of frustration-aggression theory.	d. catharsis
_____	5. It springs from anger, and its goal is to injure.	e. displacement
_____	6. Many psychologists favor this as an alternative to censorship.	f. social contagion
		g. media awareness training
_____	7. Positive, helpful social behavior.	h. social learning theory
_____	8. A perspective that emphasizes the importance of modeling.	i. frustration
_____	9. It aims to injure but only as a means to some other end.	j. Dollard
_____	10. Amplifies aggression in groups.	k. Freud
_____	11. Stated that a primitive death urge accounts for aggression.	l. Bandura
_____	12. Our feeling that we are less well off than others to whom we compare ourselves.	m. instinctive behavior
_____	13. The leading proponent of social learning theory.	n. social scripts
_____	14. Emotional release.	o. instrumental aggression
_____	15. Culturally provided mental instructions for how to act.	

TRUE-FALSE REVIEW

Circle T if the statement is true and F if it is false.

T F   1. Aggression is any behavior that results in harm coming to another person.

T F   2. All psychologists agree that aggression is maladaptive and self-destructive.

T F   3. Hostile aggression seeks to injure but only as a means to some other end.

T F   4. Sigmund Freud theorized that human nature has within it a primitive death urge.

T F   5. Both laboratory experiments and police data indicate that alcohol unleashes aggression when people are provoked.

T F   6. The catharsis hypothesis assumes that aggression is produced by frustration.

T F   7. Half of identical twins of convicted criminals also have criminal records.

T F   8. In 65 percent of homicides, the assailant and/or the victim had been drinking.

T F   9. Mice have been bred for aggressiveness.

T F 10. Seeing a hunting rifle primes aggressive thoughts for hunters but not for nonhunters.

T F 11. Happiness tends to be lower and crime rates higher in nations with large income inequality.

T F 12. The term *relative deprivation* refers to the tendency to adapt to a given level of stimulation and thus to react to changes from that level.

T F 13. After a big basketball game between archrivals, testosterone levels rise in the winning fans and fall in the losing fans.

T F 14. Social learning theory denies that frustration plays any role in aggression.

T F 15. When Washington, D.C., adopted a law restricting handgun possession, the number of gun-related murders and suicides dropped about 25 percent.

T F 16. Research has indicated that violent acts are more likely to occur on hot days.

T F 17. Research indicates that three in four stranger rapes and nearly all acquaintance rapes go unreported to the police.

T F 18. In one survey of fourth graders, the majority of boys and the majority of girls reported that their favorite video games were violent ones.

161

T F 19. Most abused children eventually become criminals or abusive parents.

T F 20. In one survey of prison inmates, 4 out of 10 said they had attempted specific crimes they had seen on television.

T F 21. Correlational studies but not laboratory experiments indicate that viewing aggression leads to aggression.

T F 22. After viewing violence, people offer more hostile explanations for others' behavior.

T F 23. After a war, a nation's murder rate tends to jump.

T F 24. High levels of serotonin are often found among violence-prone children and adults.

T F 25. Reward for nonaggression is more effective than punishment for aggression in reducing violence.

MULTIPLE-CHOICE PRACTICE TEST

Circle the correct letter.

1. According to the text, aggression always

   a. causes physical pain
   b. involves intent to harm someone
   c. involves emotional arousal
   d. is committed by someone who has been deliberately provoked

2. The murders committed by mobster "hit men" provide an example of

   a. emotional aggression
   b. silent aggression
   c. how catharsis can reduce aggression
   d. instrumental aggression

3. Research on biological influences on aggression indicates that

   a. animals can be bred for aggressiveness
   b. neural influences facilitate animal aggression but not human aggression
   c. human aggression is instinctive
   d. there are no biochemical influences on aggression in humans

4. Evolutionary psychologists suggest that the high level of male-male aggression across human history can be understood in terms of

   a. the universal experience of frustration
   b. relative deprivation
   c. the adaptive value of aggression
   d. observational learning

5. Which of the following is false?

   a. Animals' "social" aggression and "silent" aggression seem to involve the same brain region
   b. Alcohol enhances violence by reducing people's self-awareness
   c. Low levels of serotonin are often found in the violence-prone
   d. "Hostile" aggression springs from emotions such as anger

6. Research on the effects of televised violence indicates that

   a. viewing violence produces an increase in aggression
   b. viewing violence produces catharsis and thus a reduction in aggression
   c. there is no relationship between viewing aggression and behaving aggressively
   d. viewing violence increases aggression in adolescents but not in children

7. What criticism has been leveled against instinct theory as an explanation for human aggression?

   a. it is an example of naming but not explaining social behavior
   b. research has indicated no clear biological influences on aggression
   c. it necessarily implies that aggression is adaptive
   d. it misinterprets correlation as evidence for causation

8. Compared to prisoners convicted of nonviolent crimes, those convicted of planned and unprovoked violent crimes tend to

   a. be first-borns
   b. have authoritarian attitudes
   c. be older
   d. have higher testosterone levels

9. The text suggests that one reason Britain has a murder rate lower than the United States' is because Britain

   a. has a lower average temperature
   b. has a lower unemployment rate
   c. bans handguns
   d. has a less congested population

10. In brain scans of men with antisocial conduct disorder, Adrian Raine and his colleagues found that the _____ was _____ than normal.

    a. prefrontal cortex; smaller   c. amydala; smaller
    b. prefrontal cortex; larger   d. amydala; larger

11. Research on rape in the United States suggests that

    a. 9 in 10 stranger rapes are not reported to police
    b. 18 percent of women in one survey reported an experience that met the legal definition of rape
    c. acquaintance rapes are typically reported to the police
    d. the rape rate is lower than in most other industrialized countries

12. In a revision of frustration-aggression theory, Berkowitz theorized that

    a. frustration produces escape more often than aggression
    b. aggression is learned through a modeling effect
    c. aggressive cues can release bottled-up anger
    d. frustration is instinctive

13. To know whether people are frustrated we need to know

    a. their expectations and their attainments
    b. their level of deprivation and their power
    c. their wants and their intelligence
    d. their needs and their age

14. Various commentators have suggested that Americans' eagerness to attack Iraq is best understood in terms of

    a. relative deprivation   c. a culture of honor
    b. media awareness training   d. displaced aggression

15. According to _____, emotional arousal plus anticipated consequences provides the formula for aggression.

    a. ethological theory   c. frustration-aggression theory
    b. catharsis theory   d. social learning theory

16. According to Bandura, a social learning theorist,

    a. frustration plays no role in aggression
    b. observing aggressive models promotes aggression
    c. the hydraulic model offers the best explanation for aggression
    d. hostile aggression is instinctive and instrumental aggression is learned

17. In studying the capacity of electric shock to elicit attack behavior in rats, Nathan Azrin and his colleagues found that

   a. the shocked animals were choosy about their attack targets and would attack only other animals of the same species
   b. increasing the shock resulted in attempts on the part of the rats to escape rather than to attack
   c. the shock-attack reaction was clearly present in many different species
   d. shocks alone and not other aversive stimuli elicited attack

18. Which of the following is false?

   a. Pain heightens aggressiveness in animals but not in humans
   b. Being insulted by another is especially conducive to aggression
   c. In laboratory experiments heat triggers retaliative actions
   d. According to social learning theory, aggression is most likely when we are aroused and it seems safe and rewarding to aggress

19. In the Schacter and Singer experiment, which subjects felt the most anger?

   a. those who were given an adrenaline injection, were forewarned of the drug's effects, and were in the company of a euphoric person
   b. those who were given an adrenaline injection, were not forewarned of the drug's effects, and were in the company of a euphoric person
   c. those who were given an adrenaline injection, were forewarned of the drug's effects, and were in the company of a hostile person
   d. those who were given an adrenaline injection, were not forewarned of the drug's effects, and were in the company of a hostile person

20. Research clearly indicates that playing violent video games decreases

   a. prosocial behaviors
   b. levels of frustration and stress
   c. heart rate and blood pressure
   d. aggressive thinking

21. Culturally provided mental instructions for how to act in various situations are called

   a. visual heuristics   c. cognitive maps
   b. media norms   d. social scripts

22. According to the text, television's biggest effect may be that it

    a. desensitizes people to violence around them
    b. is the major cause of social violence
    c. presents an unreal picture of the world
    d. replaces other activities that people might engage in

23. Correlational research indicates that as pornography has become more widely available, the rate of reported rape has

    a. increased
    b. decreased
    c. remained unchanged
    d. increased in the short run but decreased in the long run

24. Gallup youth surveys indicate that the number of teens who believe that there is too much movie violence has _____ and the number of teens who believe that movies have become too sexually explicit has _____.

    a. increased; increased   c. decreased; increased
    b. increased; decreased   d. decreased; decreased

25. Sales rates of sexually explicit magazines such as <u>Hustler</u> and <u>Playboy</u> were positively correlated with state

    a. rape rates   c. divorce rates
    b. unemployment rates   d. child abuse rates

26. In examining the relationship between boys' viewing violence and their aggressiveness, Eron and Huesmann found that

    a. the viewing of violence at age eight was negatively correlated with aggressiveness at age nineteen
    b. the viewing of violence at age eight was positively correlated with aggressiveness at age nineteen
    c. aggressiveness at age eight was positively correlated with the viewing of violence at age nineteen
    d. Both b and c are true

27. Research indicates that American cities and areas populated by southerners have much _____ than cities and areas populated by northerners.

    a. higher White homicide rates
    b. lower White homicide rates
    c. higher Black suicide rates
    d. lower Black suicide rates

28. Research indicates that in comparison to light viewers, heavy viewers of television

    a. engage in greater prosocial behavior
    b. underestimate the number of murders that occur annually in the United States
    c. think the world is a more dangerous place
    d. tend to be more extroverted

29. Which of the following is true of findings regarding the catharsis hypothesis?

    a. The expression of angry but not instrumental aggression leads to less aggression
    b. Aggression tends to lead to heightened aggression
    c. The catharsis hypothesis has been well-supported
    d. The catharsis hypothesis is valid for adults but not for children

30. Violent pornographic films often convey a false impression that

    a. women enjoy aggressive sexual encounters
    b. women are more likely to be rape victims than are men
    c. most rapes are never reported to the police
    d. most rapes are committed by victims' dates or acquaintances

31. According to the text, the statement to a friend, "When you talk like that I feel irritated,"

    a. is, by definition, an act of angry aggression
    b. is best unsaid for it will prove frustrating to the friend and invite retaliation
    c. provides an informative, nonaggressive expression of feeling
    d. is best unsaid for while it may prove cathartic for you in the short run, it will make you
       feel more aggressive in the long run

32. The text suggests that crime rates may be higher in communities and nations with large
    income inequality because of

    a. catharsis   c. crowding
    b. displacement   d. relative deprivation

33. University men who were angered by a fellow student retaliated with much stronger shock

    a. when in groups than when alone
    b. when the experimenter was not present than when he was observing their aggression
    c. when the subject was an acquaintance than when he was a stranger
    d. if after being angered, but before delivering shock, they were exposed to mildly erotic
       stimuli

167

34. Which of the following is probably least effective in reducing aggression?

    a. Rewards for nonaggressive behavior
    b. Reducing the availability of weapons
    c. Ignoring aggressive behavior
    d. Punishing aggressive behavior

35. Which of the following cases would be an example of aggression as defined in the text?

    a. A wife deliberately belittles her husband in front of friends after he burns the pot roast
    b. A golfer accidentally hits another player with a golf ball
    c. A nurse gives a penicillin shot to a child
    d. A salesman tops his previous record by selling 50 cars in one month

36. A person kicking a cat after losing a game of checkers is displaying

    a. regression   c. relative frustration
    b. displacement   d. the weapons effect

37. Cedric and Phillip are college roommates who spend many hours each week playing violent video games. Research suggests that, compared to their peers, Cedric and Phillip are likely to

    a. be less physically aggressive   c. be more physically aggressive
    b. have lower levels of testosterone   d. have higher levels of testosterone

38. John just received a 5 percent increase in salary. However, after learning that his coworkers all received 10 percent increases, John becomes angry with his employer. We can understand John's feelings in terms of

    a. relative deprivation
    b. displacement
    c. Parkinson's second law
    d. the hydraulic model of aggression

39. As part of therapy, a clinical psychologist encourages her patients to install a punching bag in their homes to release hostility. The therapist apparently believes in

    a. social learning theory   c. the catharsis hypothesis
    b. Parkinson's second law   d. the adaptation-level phenomenon

40. Which of the following is the best example of instrumental aggression?

   a. An angry football player tackles a quarterback after he has completed a long pass
   b. A jealous wife finds her husband with another woman and shoots both of them
   c. A group of former soldiers kill the dictator of a small country for $10,000
   d. A man smashes his television set after he finds it does not work

SHORT ESSAY QUESTIONS

Answer the following questions in the space provided.

1. State the difference between hostile and instrumental aggression.

2. Discuss how aggression is biologically influenced.

3. Give an example of relative deprivation from your own life.

4. Briefly describe the social learning view of aggression.

5. Describe three aversive experiences that may heighten aggression.

6. Explain the impact of emotional arousal on aggression.

7. List two effects of viewing pornography.

8. Describe the effects of playing violent video games.

9. List three effective ways of reducing aggression.

<u>ANSWER KEY</u>

Chapter Review

1. harm
   Hostile
   Instrumental

2. instinctual
   explodes
   adaptive

3. biological
   neural
   chemistry

4. frustration
   anger
   cues

5. expectations
   Relative

6. Social
   observing
   aroused
   rewarding

7. pain
   heat
   attacked

8. interpret
   exercise
   anger
   perceptions
   aggression
   media awareness

9. catharsis
   increase
   desensitize
   conception
   games

10. groups
    amplify

11. reduced
    heightened

12. aversive
    rewarding
    Punishment

13. weapons

Matching Terms

1. e
2. i
3. m
4. j
5. a
6. g
7. b

8. h
9. o
10. f
11. k
12. c
13. l
14. d
15. n

True-False Review

1.	F		14.	F
2.	F		15.	T
3.	F		16.	T
4.	T		17.	T
5.	T		18.	T
6.	F		19.	F
7.	T		20.	T
8.	T		21.	F
9.	T		22.	T
10.	F		23.	T
11.	T		24.	F
12.	F		25.	T
13.	T			

Multiple-Choice Practice Test

1.	b		21.	d
2.	d		22.	d
3.	a		23.	a
4.	c		24.	d
5.	a		25.	a
6.	a		26.	b
7.	a		27.	a
8.	d		28.	c
9.	c		29.	b
10.	a		30.	a
11.	b		31.	c
12.	c		32.	d
13.	a		33.	a
14.	d		34.	d
15.	d		35.	a
16.	b		36.	b
17.	c		37.	c
18.	a		38.	a
19.	d		39.	c
20.	a		40.	c

CHAPTER 11

ATTRACTION AND INTIMACY

After completing your study of this chapter you should be able to:

1. Discuss the role of proximity and physical attractiveness in initial attraction.

2. Discuss research findings on the role of similarity in friendship, and describe how liking is usually mutual.

3. Explain the reward theory of attraction.

4. Describe the nature of passionate love, and identify cultural, personality, and gender variations in love.

5. Discuss the nature of companionate love.

6. Identify the different attachment styles that characterize interpersonal relationships.

7. Discuss the importance of equity and self-disclosure in close relationships.

8. Identify several predictors of a stable marriage, and describe the detachment process.

CHAPTER REVIEW

Supply the words necessary to complete each of the following statements.

1. People have a need to _____, that is, to connect with others in enduring close relationships.

WHAT LEADS TO FRIENDSHIP AND ATTRACTION?

2. A powerful predictor of whether any two people are friends is their sheer
   _____ to each other. It provides people with the opportunity for
   _____ and thus to discover their similarities and to feel each other's
   liking. Even the _____ of interacting with another can boost
   liking. Research also indicates that mere repeated _____ tends to
   increase attraction.

3. A second determinant of one's initial liking for another is physical
   _____. The _____ phenomenon is the tendency
   for people to pair off with others who are about as attractive as themselves. Research
   indicates the presence of a strong physical-attractiveness
   _____: the assumption that what is beautiful is
   _____. Evolutionary psychologists suggest that males prefer female
   characteristics that signify _____ capacity. Females prefer males
   who have high _____.

4. Acquaintances are likely to develop a friendship if there is _____ of
   beliefs, attitudes, and values. Little support has been found for _____,
   the supposed tendency for each person to complete what is missing in the other.
   Apparently _____ rarely attract.

5. We are also likely to develop friendships with people who _____ us.
   This is particularly true when we do not attribute the other's flattery to some ingratiating
   motive, when we have recently been deprived of _____, and when
   the other's praise _____ earlier criticism.

6. We like those who _____ us or those who are associated with
   _____ feelings.

WHAT IS LOVE?

7. Robert Sternberg views love as a triangle whose three sides are _____,
   intimacy, and _____.

8. _____ love is a state of intense longing for union with another.
   Such love often includes elation and gloom, exhilaration and misery.

9. The two-factor theory of emotion states that arousal X its _____ = emotion.
   Thus any arousal can intensify passionate feelings provided one can attribute some of the
   arousal to a _____ stimulus.

10. Most cultures do have a concept of _____ love. But in some cultures,
    notably those practicing arranged marriages, love tends to _____ marriage.

Studies of men and women have found that _____ tend to fall in love more readily.

11. _____ love is the affection we feel for those with whom our lives are deeply intertwined. Such love thrives when a relationship is _____ and mutually rewarding.

WHAT ENABLES CLOSE RELATIONSHIPS?

12. From infancy to old age, _____ are central to human life. In terms of specific style, _____ individuals find it easy to get close to others. _____ attachments are marked by a sense of one's own unworthiness, ambivalence, and possessiveness. _____ individuals may be either dismissing or fearful.

13. We exchange rewards by an _____ principle. It states that what people receive from a relationship should be _____ to what they contribute to it. Tit-for-tat exchanges seem to increase people's liking for one another when their relationship is relatively _____ but diminish liking when the two seek true _____. Still, relationships are likely to endure when both partners feel it to be equitable.

14. Intimacy is fostered by reciprocal _____ in which we drop our masks and gradually let ourselves be known as we are. Partners who most reveal themselves to each other tend to express _____ satisfaction with their relationship.

HOW DO RELATIONSHIPS END?

15. Divorce risk is lower for those who marry after age _____, are well-_____, and are _____ committed. As an alternative to divorce, some people cope with a failing relationship by exhibiting _____, optimistically waiting for conditions to improve. Others passively allow the relationship to deteriorate. Still others _____ their concerns and take active steps to improve the relationship.

MATCHING TERMS

Write the letter of the term on the right before the appropriate number on the left.

_____   1. A strategy to gain another's favor.

_____   2. The need to connect with others in enduring, close relationships.

_____   3. Stimuli are rated more positively after being shown repeatedly.

_____   4. Liking people who are associated with good feelings.

_____   5. What is beautiful is good.

_____   6. This fosters intimacy.

_____   7. Outcomes are in proportion to inputs.

_____   8. The affection we feel for those with whom our lives are deeply intertwined.

_____   9. One of the most powerful predictors of whether two people are friends.

_____   10. People choose partners who are about as attractive as they are.

_____   11. Intense longing for union with another.

_____   12. Our tendency to like what we associate with ourselves.

_____   13. Characteristic ways of thinking about relationships.

a. equity

b. proximity

c. mere-exposure effect

d. physical-attractiveness stereotype

e. internal working models

f. implicit egotism

g. ingratiation

h. reward principle

i. passionate love

j. self-disclosure

k. companionate love

l. need to belong

m. matching phenomenon

Circle T if the statement is true and F if it is false.

T F 1. Merely anticipating that we will interact with someone increases liking of that person.

T F 2. The happiest couples are those who idealize one another, even seeing their partners more positively than their partners see themselves.

T F 3. Cognitive dissonance theory provides the most popular theory of social attraction.

T F 4. Equity is a condition in which people receive equal outcomes from a relationship.

T F 5. One experiment found that tit-for-tat exchanges actually diminished liking when two people sought true friendship.

T F 6. College students who evaluated strangers in a pleasant room liked them better than did those who did their evaluations in an uncomfortably hot room.

T F 7. One powerful predictor of whether any two people are friends is their proximity.

T F 8. Novel stimuli are rated more negatively after being shown repeatedly.

T F 9. America's dentists are almost twice as likely to be named Dennis as Jerry or Walter.

T F 10. Physically attractive men and women tend to be looked on by others as colder, dumber, and less moral than plainer people.

T F 11. Destructive acts harm relationships more than constructive acts build them.

T F 12. To be really attractive is to be perfectly average.

T F 13. A 17-year-old girl's facial attractiveness is a weak predictor of her attractiveness at age 30.

T F 14. Months or years later, people recall more pain over spurning someone's love than over having been spurned.

T F 15. Research strongly supports the popular idea that opposites attract.

T F 16. We are more attracted to someone who likes us from the start than to someone who likes us after initially disliking us.

T F 17. There is strong agreement both within and across cultures about who is and who is not attractive.

T F 18. In experiments, people who are left out of a simple game of ball tossing feel deflated and stressed.

T F 19. Men are more likely than women are to initiate the breakup of a premarital romance.

T F 20. Bad moods affect our thinking and memory more than do good moods.

T F 21. Married partners who do exciting things together report the best relationships.

T F 22. Only 4 in 10 infants exhibit secure attachment.

T F 23. The two-factor theory of emotion states that love is a product of jealousy and ecstasy.

T F 24. Researchers have found that women are often more willing to disclose their fears and weaknesses than are men.

T F 25. People who live in a small town or on a farm are less likely to divorce.

MULTIPLE-CHOICE PRACTICE TEST

Circle the correct letter.

1. The need to belong and to form close interpersonal relationships

   a. is at the core of our existence and thus is characteristic of people everywhere
   b. is largely a 20th-century motive that is most evident in industrialized societies
   c. is a learned motive serving our more fundamental need for self-esteem
   d. conflicts with our more basic need to survive

2. The concept of romantic love is present

   a. only in individualistic societies
   b. only in affluent societies
   c. only in cultures in which there are clear differences in gender roles
   d. in most cultures

3. In his studies of ostracism, Kipling Williams found that

    a. even experiencing "cyber-ostracism" by faceless people whom one will never meet has a negative impact
    b. ostracism has a negative impact only if one feels excluded by family or close friends
    c. being excluded has no effect on people of high status
    d. only people in western cultures use acts of ostracism to regulate social behavior

4. Our desire to return a favor is best explained in terms of the

    a. complementarity hypothesis
    b. equity rule
    c. matching phenomenon
    d. mere-exposure effect

5. Reward theory states that

    a. rewards foster romantic but not companionate love
    b. companionate love is fostered by long periods of separation
    c. flattery always leads to increased liking
    d. we like those people who are associated with good feelings

6. Which of the following observations is supported by the research on social attraction?

    a. familiarity breeds fondness
    b. opposites attract
    c. beauty times brains equals a constant
    d. absence makes the heart grow fonder

7. The mere-exposure effect provides one possible explanation for

    a. why proximity leads to liking
    b. why similarity leads to liking
    c. the equity phenomenon
    d. the matching phenomenon

8. In a study of arranged versus love-based marriages in India, researchers found that

    a love-based marriages were more likely to survive
    b. those in arranged marriages experienced reactance and never felt feelings of love for their spouse
    c. after five years of marriage, those in love-based marriages reported diminished feelings of love whereas those in arranged marriages reported more love
    d. those in love-based marriages were more likely to demonstrate the disclosure reciprocity effect

9. Based on research presented in the text, if you go out on a blind date you would be most influenced by your date's

   a. open-mindedness
   b. sense of humor
   c. physical attractiveness
   d. sincerity

10. The finding that people pair off with others who are equally as attractive is known as

   a. the matching phenomenon
   b. complementarity
   c. the reciprocity effect
   d. Gause's law

11. Which of the following statements seems to be true based on research on social attraction?

   a. What is beautiful is judged to be good
   b. What is familiar is judged to be boring
   c. What is unique is judged to be valuable
   d. What is average is judged to be unattractive

12. The evolutionary perspective suggests that females are most attracted to males who show

   a. empathy, nurturance, and self-sacrifice
   b. similarity in beliefs, attitudes, and values
   c. an ability to provide and protect resources
   d. high self-esteem, extroversion, and self-efficacy

13. According to the text, differences in the psychological characteristics of attractive and unattractive people are

   a. innate
   b. in the eye of the beholder and really do not exist
   c. the result of self-fulfilling prophecies
   d. an example of how the researcher's values may determine the outcome of research

14. When shown a picture of an average young woman, men who had been watching three beautiful women on a television show rated her as _____ than did men who had not been watching the program.

   a. more attractive
   b. less attractive
   c. more intelligent
   d. less intelligent

15. Theodore Newcomb's study of unacquainted male transfer students who roomed together in a boarding house at the University of Michigan indicated that

    a. those whose attitudes and interests were initially most similar were most likely to form close friendships
    b. those whose attitudes and interests were initially complementary were most likely to form close friendships
    c. similar students formed friendships initially but, as the weeks passed, complementary students began to form friendships that turned out to be the most lasting
    d. friendships were initially formed within the boarding house but as time passed, they dissolved and were replaced by more lasting relationships with students living elsewhere

16. In terms of adult attachment styles, people with a _____ attachment seem to be possessive and jealous, whereas individuals with a _____ attachment distrust others.

    a. secure; insecure
    b. preoccupied; dismissive
    c. fearful; preoccupied
    d. dismissive fearful

17. According to Bartholomew and Horowitz's attachment model, people with a preoccupied attachment have a _____ image of self and a _____ image of others.

    a. positive; positive
    b. negative; positive
    c. positive; negative
    d. negative; negative

18. Research on equity in interpersonal relationships suggests that

    a. a marriage contract is more likely to undermine than enhance the couple's love
    b. tit-for-tat exchanges decrease people's liking for one another in business relationships
    c. the principle is innate
    d. following the principle increases liking between males but decreases liking between females

19. French students' least favorite letter among the letters of the alphabet is

    a. the least frequent letter in the French language
    b. the hardest letter to draw
    c. the last letter of the alphabet
    d. the hardest letter to pronounce

20. Studies of the impact of the Internet on social relationships indicate that

    a. most people experience the Internet to be social isolating
    b. people show less liking for people whom they have conversed with online for 20 minutes than those met for the same time face to face
    c. friendships and romantic relationships that form on the Internet are more likely to last for at least two years
    d. people perceive off-line relationships to be more important and close than Internet friendships

21. People seem to have a lower risk of divorce if they

    a. had parents who divorced
    b. live in a large town or city
    c. cohabited before marriage
    d. are religiously committed

22. The idea that we are attracted to people who are in some ways different from us is an essential aspect of the

    a. companionate love hypothesis
    b. matching phenomenon
    c. complementarity hypothesis
    d. reward theory of attraction

23. Research suggests we may be most attracted to the person who

    a. has always said only positive things about us
    b. once said negative things about us but now evaluates us positively
    c. once said positive things but now evaluates us negatively
    d. generally says negative things about us but occasionally says something positive

24. Robert Sternberg views love as a triangle whose three sides include all the following components except

    a. friendship
    b. commitment
    c. intimacy
    d. passion

25. Compared to North Americans, Asians may be less vulnerable to disillusionment in love relationships because they

    a. are less susceptible to relative deprivation and to the adaptation-level phenomenon
    b. are more likely to substitute ludus for eros
    c. experience a greater variety of emotionally arousing situations that are steered into passionate love
    d. are less focused on personal feelings and more concerned with practical aspects of social attachments

26. According to two-factor theory, emotion is a result of

    a. motives and thoughts   c. nature and nurture
    b. rewards and punishments   d. arousal and a label

27. Compared to men who were interviewed on a low, solid bridge, men interviewed on a narrow, wobbly bridge liked a

    a. female interviewer more   c. female interviewer less
    b. male interviewer more   d. male interviewer less

28. Which of the following is true?

    a. Good health increases happiness more than bad health decreases it
    b. There are more words for positive emotions than for negative emotions
    c. Destructive acts harm close relationships more than constructive acts build them
    d. A good reputation is easier to acquire than a bad one

29. Studies of men and women falling in and out of love have revealed that men tend to

    a. fall more readily in love and more slowly out of love
    b. fall more readily in love and more readily out of love
    c. fall more slowly in love and more slowly out of love
    d. fall more slowly in love and more readily out of love

30. Which of the following is true of self-disclosure?

    a. Disclosure begets disclosure
    b. A person who engages in self-disclosure is perceived as anxious
    c. A person who engages in self-disclosure is perceived as manipulative
    d. Self-disclosure leads to infatuation but not to true love

31. Which of the following is true?

    a. Companionate love typically leads to romantic love
    b. Self-disclosure reduces feelings of romantic love
    c. Companionate love is more likely to endure when both partners feel it to be equitable
    d. Spouses who pray together are more likely to report conflict in their marriage

32. An employee who feels underpaid may demand an increase in wages or exert less effort at his or her task. This behavior is an

    a. attempt to restore equity
    b. attempt to achieve complementarity
    c. example of the matching phenomenon
    d. example of the overexposure effect

33. Tom, who tends to be extroverted, has just moved into the dormitory at Federal College. He is most likely to make friends with

    a. Bill, his next-door neighbor
    b. John, a chemistry major who lives across campus
    c. Michael, an introvert who lives on the next floor
    d. Stuart, a student who lives off campus and who loves dogs

34. Jee-Seon, who is attractive, very intelligent, and high in social status marries Dan who is also attractive, very intelligent, and high in social status. Their relationship is best understood as an example of

    a. the ingratiation effect   c. the mere-exposure effect
    b. complementarity   d. the matching phenomenon

35. Some years ago, a mysterious student enveloped in a big, black bag began attending a speech class at a state university. While the teacher knew the "Black Bag's" identity, the other students did not. As the semester progressed, the students' attitude toward the Black Bag changed from hostility to curiosity to friendship. What may best explain the students' change in attitude?

    a. Exposure breeds liking
    b. Stress produces affiliation
    c. Boredom breeds a liking for the novel
    d. Similarity attracts

36. Maria, a talkative, extraverted, young woman, is strongly attracted to Ronald, a quiet, introverted, middle-aged man. Mary's attraction to Ronald reflects

    a. implicit egotism   c. the equity principle
    b. the matching phenomenon   d. complementarity

37. You overhear a casual acquaintance express approval of you in the coffee shop. You are most likely to think well of that acquaintance if

    a. you learned an hour earlier that you had received an average grade on a history test
    b. you learned an hour earlier that you had failed a chemistry test
    c. the acquaintance is unattractive
    d. the acquaintance is engaged to be married

38. Phyllis tends to be possessive and jealous in relating to Mark, her boyfriend. She has repeatedly broken up with him and becomes very emotional when discussing conflicts with him. Phyllis's relationship with Mark demonstrates _____ attachment.

   a. bipolar
   b. preoccupied
   c. dismissive
   d. fearful

39. Bill and Sara's relationship becomes progressively more intimate as each engages in a bit more self-revelation in response to the other's self-disclosure. Their relationship is marked by the _____ effect.

   a. disclosure reciprocity
   b. mutual disinhibition
   c. reciprocal disinhibition
   d. reciprocal intimacy

40. A stranger rides the same bus you do to school every day. According to the mere-exposure effect, as the days pass you will come to view the stranger

   a. as merely another student
   b. more unfavorably
   c. more critically
   d. more favorably

SHORT ESSAY QUESTIONS

Answer the following questions in the space provided.

1. List four powerful influences on liking and friendship.

2. Why does proximity promote friendship?

3. What is the physical-attractiveness stereotype?

4. What is complementarity? What does research indicate regarding it?

5. Describe the reward theory of attraction.

6. How does the two-factor theory of emotion explain passionate love?

7. Compare and contrast passionate love with companionate love.

8. Explain the equity principle, and discuss its relevance to friendship and love.

9. Discuss the causes and effects of self-disclosure.

10. Identify four factors that are associated with a lower risk of divorce.

Chapter Review

1. belong

2. proximity
   interaction
   anticipation
   exposure

3. attractiveness
   matching
   stereotype
   good
   reproductive
   status

4. similarity
   complementarity
   opposites

5. like
   approval
   reverses

6. reward
   good

7. passion
   commitment

8. Passionate

9. label
   romantic

10. romantic
    follow
    men

11. Companionate
    intimate

12. attachments
    secure
    Preoccupied
    Avoidant

13. equity
    proportional
    formal
    friendship

14. self-disclosure
    most

15. 20
    educated
    religiously
    loyalty
    voice

Matching Terms

1. g
2. l
3. c
4. h
5. d
6. j

7. a
8. k
9. b
10. m
11. i
12. f
13. e

True-False Review

1.	T		14.	T
2.	T		15.	F
3.	F		16.	F
4.	F		17.	T
5.	T		18.	T
6.	T		19.	F
7.	T		20.	T
8.	F		21.	T
9.	T		22.	F
10.	F		23.	F
11.	T		24.	T
12.	T		25.	T
13.	T			

Multiple-Choice Practice Test

1.	a		21.	d
2.	d		22.	c
3.	a		23.	b
4.	b		24.	a
5.	d		25.	d
6.	a		26.	d
7.	a		27.	a
8.	c		28.	c
9.	c		29.	a
10.	a		30.	a
11.	a		31.	c
12.	c		32.	a
13.	c		33.	a
14.	b		34.	d
15.	a		35.	a
16.	b		36.	d
17.	b		37.	b
18.	a		38.	b
19.	a		39.	a
20.	c		40.	d

CHAPTER 12

HELPING

CHAPTER OBJECTIVES

After completing your study of this chapter you should be able to:

1. Define *altruism*.

2. Describe how social-exchange theory explains helping behavior.

3. Identify two social norms that may motivate helping.

4. Describe how evolutionary psychology accounts for helping.

5. Discuss evidence for genuine altruism.

6. Describe situational influences that affect helping.

7. Identify personal influences that affect helping.

8. Discuss how we can increase helping.

CHAPTER REVIEW

Supply the words necessary to complete each of the following statements.

1. Altruism is a motive to increase another's _____ without conscious regard
   for one's _____.

WHY DO WE HELP?

2. Social-exchange theory states that helping, like other social behaviors, is guided by social
   _____ in which we aim to maximize our _____
   and minimize our _____. Rewards for helping may be either

_____ (for example, social approval) or _____
(for example, reducing one's own distress).

3. People are _____ willing to help after transgressing, apparently in order to relieve private _____ and to restore a positive public image. People who are in a _____ mood also tend to be altruistic especially when being helpful is a way of altering their mood. This "feel bad-do good" effect is generally not found when people are angry or experiencing self-focused _____. Finally, people who are in a _____ mood are consistently more helpful.

4. Researchers have identified two social norms that seem to motivate altruism. The _____ norm is an expectation that people will help, not hurt, those who have helped them. The norm operates most effectively as people respond _____ to deeds earlier done for them. The social-_____ norm is an expectation that people will help those needing help. We apply the norm selectively by giving aid to those who _____ it. In time of need, women receive _____ offers of help than men do, especially from men.

5. Evolutionary psychology contends that the essence of life is gene _____ and thus we are programmed to be selfish. However, two forms of helping that are favored by natural selection are _____ protection and _____. Most evolutionary psychologists believe that, since people are born selfish, we must _____ altruism.

6. The three theories of helping _____ one another in offering different levels of explanation. Yet each is vulnerable to charges of being speculative and of merely explaining-by-_____. Psychologist Daniel Batson believes that seeing someone in distress may lead us to feel _____ as well as distress and so our helping may be motivated by genuine _____.

WHEN WILL WE HELP?

7. As the number of bystanders at an emergency increases, any given bystander is less likely to _____ the incident, less likely to _____ it as an emergency, and less likely to assume _____ for taking action. "_____ fatigue" and "sensory _____" help to explain why those in large cities are less helpful than country people.

8. People are likely to help after seeing someone else _____ and when they are not in a _____. We are most likely to help those who are _____ to us in both dress and beliefs.

WHO WILL HELP?

9. Early research found only _____ relationships between personality variables and helping. More recently, personality researchers have found that those high in positive _____, empathy, and _____ are most likely to be concerned and helpful. The _____ of the person and situation is clearly seen in research comparing the helpfulness of males and females. _____ faith predicts long-term altruism, for example, in volunteerism and charitable contributions.

HOW CAN WE INCREASE HELPING?

10. One way to promote helping is to _____ those factors that inhibit helping. According to the decision tree, assisting people to _____ an incident correctly, and to assume _____ for intervening, should increase their involvement. Research shows that _____ asking people for help and making them more _____-aware promotes altruism.

11. Reprimands and the door-in-the-_____ technique promote helping by evoking _____ feelings and concern for one's self-image.

12. We can also _____ moral inclusion. Research indicates that television's prosocial _____ have even greater effects on children than its antisocial ones. Children and adults also learn by _____.

13. The _____ effect suggests that we not use excessive rewards or threats in socializing altruism. If people are provided with just enough justification to help, they will view themselves as _____ persons and be more helpful. Finally, students who have heard about _____ on altruism are more helpful.

MATCHING TERMS

Write the letter of the term on the right before the appropriate number on the left.

_____ 1. An expectation that people will help those needing help.

_____ 2. The classic illustration of altruism.

_____ 3. A person is less likely to provide help when others are present.

_____ 4. Seeing another's suffering may produce this.

_____ 5. Helping that promotes gene survival.

_____ 6. Concern for one's self-image makes this effective.

_____ 7. The mutual support and cooperation enabled by a social network.

_____ 8. May prevent people who have helped from feeling altruistic.

_____ 9. The motivation to increase one's own welfare.

_____ 10. An effective means of socializing altruism.

_____ 11. Overestimating others' ability to read our emotions.

_____ 12. An expectation that people will help, not hurt, those who have helped them.

_____ 13. Perceiving certain individuals as outside the boundary within which one applies rules of fairness.

a. door-in-the-face technique

b. overjustification effect

c. bystander effect

d. egoism

e. kin selection

f. moral exclusion

g. social-responsibility norm

h. reciprocity norm

i. social capital

j. modeling

k. the Good Samaritan

l. empathy

m. illusion of transparency

TRUE-FALSE REVIEW

Circle T if the statement is true and F if it is false.

T F   1. When exposed to hypocrites, children imitate: they say what the model says and do what the model does.

T F   2. According to social norms theory, we use a "minimax" strategy in relating to others.

T F   3. Psychologists are in agreement that all our behavior is ultimately aimed at our own welfare.

T F   4. Empathy sometimes fuels injustice and indifference to the larger common good.

T F   5. The social-responsibility norm is the expectation that people will help those who have helped them.

T F   6. Evolutionary psychology maintains that the essence of life is gene survival.

T F   7. Compared to those in nonurban areas, people in big cities are less willing to do small favors.

T F   8. Religious commitment is not correlated with long-term helping.

T F   9. In contrast to the other theories of altruism, social norms theory is speculative and after-the-fact.

T F 10. As the number of bystanders increases, any given bystander is less likely to interpret an incident as an emergency.

T F 11. Difficulty in choosing the form that assistance should take is one of the three important factors contributing to the bystander effect.

T F 12. Men more frequently help attractive women than those they see as unattractive.

T F 13. Female helpers are more likely to assist female victims than male victims.

T F 14. People consistently help those of the same race more readily than those of a different race.

T F 15. When we feel guilty we are more likely to help those around us.

T F 16. People in India support the social-responsibility norm more strongly than do people in western countries.

T F 17. Self-focused grief promotes altruism.

T F 18. Happiness makes people self-focused and thus less willing to help.

T F 19. Compared to fraternal twins, genetically identical twins are noticeably more mutually supportive.

T F 20. When faced with potentially dangerous situations in which strangers need help, men are more likely to help than are women.

T F 21. Helping increases when one expects to meet the victim and witnesses again.

T F 22. Research indicated that participants who had just completed a biographical questionnaire were more willing to help.

T F 23. The door-in-the-face technique is a strategy for increasing helping.

T F 24. Research indicates that television's prosocial models actually have greater effects on viewers than its antisocial models do.

T F 25. One of the most effective ways of teaching altruism is through utilizing the overjustification effect.

MULTIPLE-CHOICE PRACTICE TEST

Circle the correct letter.

1. According to the text, the classic illustration of altruism is provided by

   a. the Kitty Genovese case
   b. the parable of the Good Samaritan
   c. the parable of the Prodigal Son
   d. President Lincoln's Emancipation Proclamation

2. *Social economics* is a term most closely associated with

   a. social norms theory
   b. evolutionary psychology
   c. social-exchange theory
   d. the decision tree

3. According to social-exchange theory we will help when

   a. the benefits are external and the costs are internal
   b. the benefits are greater than the costs
   c. the benefits and costs are proportional
   d. the benefits are smaller than the costs

4. According to Daniel Batson, genuine altruism may have its basis in feelings of

   a. happiness
   b. sadness
   c. guilt
   d. empathy

5. The misinterpretations of emotional states involved in the bystander effect are fed by

   a. an illusion of transparency
   b. an illusion of control
   c. illusory correlation
   d. the foot-in-the-door phenomenon

6. The social-responsibility norm is the expectation that people will

   a. help those needing help
   b. help those who have helped them
   c. assume responsibility for helping their parents
   d. assume responsibility for correcting past mistakes

7. According to sociologist Alvin Gouldner, a universal moral code is

   a. a norm of reciprocity
   b. a norm of social responsibility
   c. kin selection
   d. a norm of restitution

8. Altruism is to _____ as egoism is to _____.

   a. reciprocity norm; empathy
   b. self-esteem; need for achievement
   c. another's welfare; one's own welfare
   d. evolutionary psychology; social exchange theory

9. According to the text, one possible reason why people in big cities are less helpful is that

   a. they have not internalized the norm of social responsibility
   b. they are busier than those living in small towns
   c. they have a greater number of selfish genes
   d. reciprocity does not work as well in big cities as it does in small, isolated groups

10. A Gallup poll found that being engaged with a faith community was
    _____ with volunteering.

    a. negatively correlated
    b. uncorrelated
    c. positively correlated
    d. positively correlated for women and negatively correlated for men

11. According to Batson and his colleagues, one of the limitations of empathy is that it can

    a. foster negative attitudes toward stigmatized groups
    b. fuel aggression
    c. produce favoritism
    d. decrease cooperation

12. According to the text, which theory of altruism proposes two types of altruism: a tit-for-tat reciprocal exchange, and a more unconditional helpfulness?

    a. social norms theory   c. social-exchange theory
    b. evolutionary psychology   d. all of the these

13. Latane and Darley attempted to explain people's failure to intervene in cases like that of Kitty Genovese in terms of

    a. a situational influence   c. a mood factor
    b. a personality trait   d. selfish genes

14. Researchers had participants fill out a questionnaire in a room either by themselves or with two strangers. When the experimenters pumped smoke through a wall vent, solitary participants

    a. noticed the smoke more quickly than did those in groups
    b. were more likely to misinterpret the smoke as being truth gas
    c. were less likely to seek help
    d. finished the questionnaire more quickly

15. What is meant by the term *bystander effect*?

    a. People are likely to gather at the scene of a serious accident
    b. People are likely to gather at the scene of a fire and hinder rescue operations
    c. People are more likely to provide aid when there are helping models present
    d. People are less likely to provide help when there are other bystanders

16. Which of the following is not one of the factors that Darley and Latane considered in analyzing the bystander effect?

    a. noticing the incident
    b. interpreting the incident as an emergency
    c. weighing the costs and benefits of helping
    d. assuming responsibility for intervening

17. Research suggests that men have been more likely than women to

   a. donate a kidney
   b. to volunteer with the Peace Corps
   c. to risk death as Holocaust rescuers
   d. None of these are true: that is, women have been equally or more likely to help in these ways

18. When participants in Darley and Latane's seizure experiment were later interviewed,

   a. most said they thought the deception used by the experimenter was justified but they would not be willing to take part in future similar experiments because of the stress
   b. most said they did not think the deception was justified but they would take part in future similar experiments
   c. most said they did not think the deception was justified and they would not take part in future similar experiments
   d. all said they thought the deception was justified and would be willing to take part in future similar experiments

19. According to the text, people in a hurry may be less willing to help because

   a. they have weighed the costs of helping and have decided they are too high
   b. they do not tune in to the person in need
   c. they tend to be selfish and primarily concerned with meeting their own needs
   d. they tend to be in a negative mood state and therefore are less likely to help

20. Researchers who have investigated the relationship between empathy and altruism

   a. agree that empathy leads to genuine altruism
   b. agree that empathy leads to helping that is egoistically motivated
   c. agree that empathy leads to pure altruism in females but not in males
   d. debate whether empathy leads to pure altruism

21. Which of the following negative moods is most likely to motivate altruism?

   a. depression   c. guilt
   b. anger   d. grief

22. Research suggests that we are especially likely to help when

   a. we are happy
   b. others are present and are doing nothing
   c. the potential recipient of our help is of the opposite sex
   d. the potential recipient of our help is of a different nationality

23. In comparison to low self-monitors, high self-monitors are especially helpful if

    a. they are led to think that helpfulness will be socially rewarded
    b. the social-responsibility norm is salient
    c. they are exposed to altruistic models
    d. they experience empathy

24. Batson found that those who attributed their helpful act to compliance rather than compassion

    a. subsequently volunteered less time to a service agency
    b. demonstrated reactance and ended up feeling more empathy for the person they helped
    c. felt guilty and responded more positively to a new request for help
    d. were subsequently more aware of the reciprocity norm

25. Rewards and costs are to _____ as gene survival is to _____.

    a. social-exchange theory; social norms theory
    b. sociobiology; social norms theory
    c. social norms theory; evolutionary psychology
    d. social-exchange theory; evolutionary psychology

26. Research has indicated that when students have been informed through a lecture of how bystanders can affect one's reactions to an emergency, the

    a. students are subsequently more likely to help someone in need
    b. students' willingness to help is unchanged because they refuse to believe that they can be influenced by other people
    c. students' willingness to help is increased for a few hours following the lecture but for no longer
    d. students' willingness to help actually decreases owing to psychological reactance

27. Research suggests that those who are high in _____ are more likely to be helpful.

    a. authoritarianism   c. extroversion
    b. self-efficacy   d. achievement motivation

28. The mutual support and cooperation enabled by a social network is referred to as

    a. kin protection   c. social capital
    b. community empathy   d. the elevation principle

29. What does research indicate regarding the role of gender difference in predicting helping?

    a. Gender is unrelated to helping
    b. Males are more helpful than females
    c. Females are more helpful than males
    d. Gender difference interacts with the situation

30. According to the text, the door-in-the-face technique works to promote altruism because people are

    a. provided a helpful model to imitate
    b. in a happy mood
    c. concerned about their self-image
    d. distracted from self-concern

31. When a solicitor for a charitable cause added the phrase, "Even a penny will help" to the request for a donation,

    a. the total number of contributors increased but the average amount of each contribution decreased
    b. both the number of contributors and the average amount of each contribution decreased
    c. both the number of contributors and the average amount of each contribution increased
    d. the total number of contributors decreased but the average amount of each contribution increased

32. In socializing altruism, we should beware of the

    a. overjustification effect   c. fundamental attribution error
    b. underjustification effect   d. foot-in-the-door effect

33. Which of the following religious teachings most clearly promotes "moral inclusion"?

    a. "Love your neighbor as yourself"
    b. "Everyone is a child of God and thus your brother or sister"
    c. "Honor your father and your mother"
    d. "An eye for an eye and a tooth for a tooth"

34. You trip over a fallen branch and sprain your ankle. According to research on the bystander effect, a stranger who sees your plight will be most likely to offer aid if there are _____ others present.

    a. no   c. four
    b. two   d. ten

35. The statement, "There is no duty more indispensable than that of returning a kindness," reflects the _____ norm.

    a. restitution   c. social-responsibility
    b. reciprocity   d. equity

36. Who of the following is least likely to help an injured pedestrian?

    a. Peter who has just found $10 in a grocery store
    b. Anita who is five minutes late for a committee meeting
    c. Carol who has just lost a dollar bill in a poker game
    d. Ralph who is five minutes early for work

37. Your roommate asks you to loan her $25 to buy her boyfriend a birthday present and you refuse. She then asks $3 to purchase a new notebook. You loan her the $3. Your roommate has successfully used the

    a. overjustification effect
    b. insufficient justification effect
    c. door-in-the-face technique
    d. foot-in-the-door technique

38. From an evolutionary perspective it would be most difficult to explain why

    a. John paid his son's hospital bill
    b. Phyllis helps her mother clean the house
    c. William helps his next-door neighbor paint his house
    d. Ruth risked her life to save a stranger from being murdered

39. Which of the following techniques should elementary schoolteachers use if they hope to promote enduring altruistic tendencies in students?

    a. show them films of heroes who risked their own welfare to help others
    b. offer a prize to the boy or girl who is most helpful to other students in a two-week period
    c. reprimand and punish any overt aggression
    d. instill a sense of patriotism

40. When his car overheated on a nearly deserted highway early one morning, elderly Mr. Hurley received help from the first passerby. One week later the same thing happened in the afternoon when traffic was heavy, and Mr. Hurley waited nearly two hours for help. This difference best illustrates

    a. the overjustification effect   c. the illusion of transparency
    b. social facilitation   d. the bystander effect

SHORT ESSAY QUESTIONS

Answer the following questions in the space provided.

1. Define *altruism*.

2. How does social-exchange theory explain helping?

3. List two social norms that may motivate helping and briefly explain each.

4. What two kinds of helping are predicted by evolutionary psychology? Give a specific example of each.

5. Explain why bystanders often inhibit helping.

6. Describe how time pressures affect helping behavior.

7. What is the relationship between personality and willingness to help?

8. Describe the relationship between religious faith and helping.

9. Discuss how we can increase helping behavior.

ANSWER KEY

Chapter Review

1. welfare
   self-interests

2. economics
   rewards
   costs
   external
   internal

3. more
   guilt
   negative
   grief
   positive

4. reciprocity
   publicly
   responsibility
   deserve
   more

5. survival
   kin
   reciprocity
   teach

6. complement
   naming
   empathy
   altruism

7. notice
   interpret
   responsibility
   Compassion
   overload

8. help
   hurry
   similar

9. modest
   emotionality
   self-efficacy
   interaction
   Religious

10. reverse
    interpret
    responsibility
    personally
    self

11. face
    guilt

12. teach
    models
    doing

13. overjustfication
    altruistic
    research

Matching Terms

1.	g	7.	i
2.	k	8.	b
3.	c	9.	d
4.	l	10.	j
5.	e	11.	m
6.	a	12.	h
		13.	f

True-False Review

1.	T	14.	F
2.	F	15.	T
3.	F	16.	T
4.	T	17.	F
5.	F	18.	F
6.	T	19.	T
7.	T	20.	T
8.	F	21.	T
9.	F	22.	T
10.	T	23.	T
11.	F	24.	T
12.	T	25.	F
13.	F		

Multiple-Choice Practice Test

1.	b	21.	c
2.	c	22.	a
3.	b	23.	a
4.	d	24.	a
5.	a	25.	d
6.	a	26.	a
7.	a	27.	b
8.	c	28.	c
9.	d	29.	d
10.	c	30.	c
11.	c	31.	c
12.	d	32.	a
13.	a	33.	b
14.	a	34.	a
15.	d	35.	b
16.	c	36.	b
17.	d	37.	c
18.	d	38.	d
19.	b	39.	a
20.	d	40.	d

CHAPTER 13

CONFLICT AND PEACEMAKING

<u>CHAPTER OBJECTIVES</u>

After completing your study of this chapter you should be able to:

1. Define *conflict* and *peace*.

2. Explain how the pursuit of self-interest can produce a social dilemma.

3. Suggest specific ways of resolving social dilemmas.

4. Describe how competition produces conflict.

5. Describe the criterion most people use to define *justice*.

6. Identify specific misperceptions that fuel conflict.

7. List the conditions under which close contact reduces hostility between opposing parties.

8. Describe how superordinate goals reduce conflict.

9. Explain how bargaining, mediation, and arbitration can be used to resolve differences between opposing parties.

10. Describe the GRIT model for reducing conflict.

<u>CHAPTER REVIEW</u>

Supply the words necessary to complete each of the following statements.

1. Conflict is a _____ incompatibility of actions or goals. _____ is a condition marked by low levels of hostility and aggression and by mutually beneficial relationships.

WHAT CREATES CONFLICT?

2. Social dilemmas such as nuclear arms, overpopulation, and natural resource depletion are the result of various parties rationally pursuing their _____ to their collective _____. The _____ Dilemma and the Tragedy of the _____ games have been used to study how well-meaning people easily become trapped in mutually destructive behavior.

3. Research with the laboratory dilemmas suggests that cooperation can be promoted by regulation, by keeping social groups _____ so that people feel responsibility for one another, by allowing people to _____ and thereby reducing mistrust, by changing the payoffs to make cooperation more rewarding, and by appeals to _____ norms.

4. _____ for scarce resources can also breed conflict. In a series of famous experiments, Sherif divided boys into two groups and found that win-_____ competition triggered outright warfare.

5. Many people believe the criterion for justice is _____, in which the distribution of rewards is in _____ to individuals' contributions. When people feel exploited, they may accept and justify their inferior position, demand _____, or attempt to restore _____ by retaliating.

6. Conflicts often contain only a small core of truly incompatible goals but are surrounded by many _____ of the other's motives and goals. Opposing parties often have _____ perceptions: Each attributes the same virtues to themselves and the same vices to the other. Such images are often self-_____. International conflicts are also fed by the evil _____-good _____ illusion.

HOW CAN PEACE BE ACHIEVED?

7. Early studies of desegregation, for example, in public housing, indicated that racial contact _____ prejudice. More recent studies show that desegregation of schools has _____ effect up racial attitudes. Contact that is prolonged, intimate, and structured to convey _____ status often reduces conflict.

8. In his boys' camp experiments, Sherif demonstrated how conflict between groups promotes _____ within groups. He introduced _____ goals to reconcile opposing groups. Similarly, replacing competitive learning situations with opportunities for _____ learning improved race relations in desegregated schools.

9. In everyday life, we often reconcile multiple _____. Bicultural people who affirm both their ethnic and mainstream identities typically have a strongly positive _____.

10. When conflicts are not intense or at an impasse, opposing parties may _____ directly, that is, seek agreement through direct negotiation. Sometimes a third-party _____ can help antagonists by replacing their win-_____ view of the conflict with a more cooperative win-_____ orientation. They can also reduce _____ and increase mutual understanding and trust. _____ is resolution of a conflict by a neutral third party who studies both sides and imposes a solution.

11. Sometimes tension is so high that genuine communication becomes impossible. In such cases, small _____ acts by one party may elicit reciprocal actions from the other. In Osgood's _____ model, one party to a conflict _____ its conciliatory intent, invites the adversary to _____, carries out several verifiable conciliatory _____, and maintains its _____ capability.

MATCHING TERMS

Write the letter of the term on the right before the appropriate number on the left.

_____ 1. Uses conciliation to reduce tension.	a. integrative agreement
_____ 2. Sherif's solution to conflict in a boys' summer camp.	b. equity
_____ 3. Reconciles conflicting parties' interests to their mutual benefit.	c. superordinate goal
_____ 4. A third party imposes a settlement.	d. mirror-image perceptions
_____ 5. On any given trial in this game, one is better off confessing.	e. Rattlers and Eagles
_____ 6. The distribution of rewards in proportion to individuals' contributions.	f. GRIT
_____ 7. Arab and Israeli views.	g. jigsaw technique
_____ 8. A cooperative learning technique used in schools.	h. equal status
_____ 9. Contact between opposing groups must be of this sort if it is to reduce conflict.	i. mediation
_____ 10. An effort to synthesize aspects of both individualism and collectivism.	j. arbitration
_____ 11. The opposing parties seek agreement through direct negotiation.	k. bargaining
_____ 12. Competition produced conflict and a common goal reduced it.	l. Prisoner's Dilemma
_____ 13. A third party facilitates communication between two opposing groups.	m. communitarianism

214

TRUE-FALSE REVIEW

Circle T if the statement is true and F if it is false.

T F   1. Conflict is always a destructive drain on human potential.

T F   2. Conflict is a perceived incompatibility of actions or goals.

T F   3. In the Prisoner's Dilemma, a person always receives the best payoff on a particular trial if he or she cooperates.

T F   4. The laboratory dilemmas tempt people to explain their own behavior dispositionally and their partners' behavior situationally.

T F   5. The Tragedy of the Commons refers to the loss of one's personal property when it is taken over by the government.

T F   6. Aronson's use of the "jigsaw" technique demonstrates how conciliation reduces conflict.

T F   7. The Prisoner's Dilemma is an example of a non-zero-sum game.

T F   8. In laboratory dilemmas people who realize that their self-serving choices are mutually destructive stop making them.

T F   9. Integrative agreements are win-win agreements that reconcile both parties' interests to their mutual benefit.

T F 10. Sherif's experiments in a boys' summer camp demonstrated how competition can produce social conflict.

T F 11. All cultures tend to define justice in terms of equity.

T F 12. Equity involves the distribution of rewards in proportion to individuals' needs.

T F 13. People with opposing views on issues such as affirmative action and immigration often differ less than they suppose.

T F 14. Conflicts often contain only a small number of truly incompatible goals.

T F 15. After reading about the commons dilemma, theater patrons littered less than those who had read about voting.

T F 16. Student exchange programs invariably improve students' attitudes toward their host countries.

215

T F 17. Results of school desegregation studies have shown that interracial contact consistently reduces prejudice.

T F 18. Sherif used arbitration to reduce conflict in the boys' summer camp.

T F 19. Cooperative learning strategies have been shown to improve race relations in desegregated schools.

T F 20. Mediation involves resolution of a conflict by a third party who studies both sides and imposes a settlement.

T F 21. The Kennedy experiment demonstrates how arbitration can reduce conflict.

T F 22. If you want to buy a new car at the best price, adopting a tough bargaining stance by opening with a very low offer typically backfires.

T F 23. GRIT uses conciliation to reduce conflict.

T F 24. The more majority members endorse multiculturalism, the more likely they are to identify with their own ethnic group and to be dismissive of outgroups.

T F 25. In laboratory games, people who are 100 percent cooperative are rarely exploited.

MULTIPLE-CHOICE PRACTICE TEST

Circle the correct letter.

1. Which of the following is true of conflict?

   a. Without conflict, people seldom face and resolve their problems
   b. Conflict always involves a real incompatibility of goals
   c. Social psychologists have studied interpersonal but not international conflict
   d. Social psychologists have not been able to study conflict in a laboratory setting

2. The Tragedy of the Commons illustrates how

   a. communism leads to economic ruin
   b. self-serving behavior leads to collective doom
   c. false stereotypes lead to social conflict
   d. superordinate goals may fail to produce cooperation in capitalistic societies

3. Before the United States began the Iraq war in 2003 it assumed the existence of a "vast underground network that would rise in support of coalition forces to assist security and law enforcement." This assumption provides an example of

    a. a mirror-image perception
    b. a non-zero-sum analysis
    c. an illusion of transparency
    d. an evil leader-good people perception

4. In non-zero-sum games,

    a. one player always wins and the other always loses
    b. one player's winnings equal the other player's losses
    c. both players may win, both may lose, or one may win and the other may lose
    d. the players' combined outcomes can never equal zero

5. The _____ the commons, the _____ responsibility each person feels for it.

    a. smaller; more   c. more important; more
    b. larger; more   d. more important; less

6. Research on laboratory dilemmas reveals that cooperation is facilitated if

    a. one person is 100 percent cooperative
    b. the opponents can communicate with each other
    c. the game is changed into a zero-sum game
    d. the size of the payoffs is increased

7. Appeals to altruistic norms

    a. have proven to be helpful in reducing social dilemmas
    b. work in resolving small-scale but not large-scale dilemmas
    c. create reactance and make people more competitive
    d. work to resolve conflict in the Prisoner's Dilemma but not in the Tragedy of the Commons

8. Sherif's experiments in a boys' summer camp demonstrated how _____ reduce conflict.

    a. appeals to altruistic norms   c. communications
    b. regulations   d. superordinate goals

9. People are likely to have high self-esteem if they have a _____ ethnic identity and a _____ mainstream cultural identity.

    a. weak; weak
    b. weak; strong
    c. strong; weak
    d. strong; strong

10. According to the text, which of the following factors impedes cross-racial contacts and friendship formation?

    a. the equity principle
    b. groupthink
    c. pluralistic ignorance
    d. deindividuation

11. According to the text, the integration of major league baseball with the arrival of Jackie Robinson included all the following factors <u>except</u>

    a. the offer of final-offer arbitration
    b. establishing equal status contact with a superordinate goal
    c. puncturing the norm of prejudice
    d. creating a perception that change is inevitable

12. When Gregory Mitchell and his colleagues asked American University students what standard of justice they would prefer if their own place on the economic ladder was unknown, they indicated that they would prefer

    a. that resources be distributed equally
    b. that resources be distributed on the basis of productivity
    c. enough priority placed on equality to meet their own needs but also some reward for productivity
    d. that goods be distributed strictly on the basis of need

13. Shared goals that necessitate cooperative effort are said to be

    a. reciprocal
    b. superordinate
    c. equitable
    d. companionate

14. The tendency of each party to a conflict to see itself as moral and peaceloving and the other as evil and aggressive is known as

    a. reciprocal illusory perceptions
    b. the fundamental attribution error
    c. illusory correlation
    d. mirror-image perception

15. According to Walter Stephan's review of the research, what has been the influence of school desegregation on racial attitudes in the United States?

   a. Overall, racial attitudes seem to have been little affected
   b. Hostility has increased
   c. Hostility has decreased
   d. Hostility has increased in the South but decreased in the North

16. Contact between opposing racial groups reduces hostility

   a. if it occurs in a competitive situation in which parties are likely to communicate with each other
   b. if the minority group is given superior status
   c. if it is structured to convey equal status
   d. between younger members of the respective groups but not between older members

17. Conflict between groups promotes _____ within groups.

   a. unity   c. concern for equity
   b. conflict   d. role confusion

18. Studies of the use of cooperative learning strategies in the schools have shown that such strategies can

   a. increase self-esteem   c. improve race relations
   b. increase liking for school d. do all of these

19. Which of the following is a cooperative learning strategy used in schools?

   a. the GRIT model   c. Prisoner's Dilemma
   b. the jigsaw technique   d. the Simulated Mediation Game

20. Bargaining tough is likely to backfire

   a. when the conflict is over a pie of fixed size
   b. when the conflict is over a pie that can shrink
   c. when females bargain tough with males
   d. in virtually every situation

21. The GRIT strategy was formulated as a plan

   a. for reversing conflict through conciliation
   b. for decreasing interracial tensions in desegregated schools
   c. to demonstrate how conflict in general can be reduced through arbitration
   d. to demonstrate how regulation can alleviate social dilemmas

22. In playing the laboratory version of Prisoner's Dilemma, a person's outcome from <u>any given decision</u> will be better if he or she

    a.   cooperates
    b.   defects
    c.   cooperates only if the other person cooperates
    d.   cooperates only if the other person defects

23. When Kaori Sato used a simulated forest to study the Commons Dilemma in a communal culture, he found

    a.   results much like those obtained in western cultures
    b.   that people were much more cooperative than in western cultures
    c.   females but not males were more cooperative than their counterparts in western cultures
    d.   adults but not children were more cooperative than their counterparts in western cultures

24. When Robyn Dawes and his colleagues gave people a short sermon about group benefits, exploitation, and ethics before they played a dilemma game,

    a.   people reacted by playing even more competitively
    b.   people were more cooperative in their play
    c.   people ignored the sermon and their play was unchanged
    d.   females were more cooperative and males were more competitive

25. A cooperative effort engaged in by two previously conflicting groups

    a.   always has the long-term effect of boosting the groups' attraction to each other
    b.   may actually increase tension between the two groups if the effort is unsuccessful
    c.   will be effective in reducing long-term tensions only if engaging in the effort was suggested by a mediator
    d.   typically reduces long-term conflict between opposing groups of males but not between opposing groups of females

26. Compared to compromises, integrative agreements are

    a.   more enduring and lead to better ongoing relationships
    b.   only reached through mediation or arbitration
    c.   only possible when perceived injustice is the cause of conflict
    d.   less likely to lead to a permanent settlement

27. We are most likely to generalize positive interracial experiences with a few individuals to a more positive attitude toward a whole outgroup if we perceive

    a. the outgroup as being as diverse as our own group
    b. the individuals as being representative of their group rather than as atypical
    c. ourselves as the only members from our own group having positive experiences with the outgroup
    d. the individuals as high in social status within the outgroup

28. In "final-offer arbitration," the third party settles a conflict by

    a. choosing between the final offers made by each side
    b. compromising between the final offers made by each side
    c. providing an integrative agreement based on final offers from each side
    d. introducing a superordinate goal

29. A key factor in determining whether people will communicate constructively and thereby correct misperceptions is

    a. their trust that the opposing side is well-intentioned
    b. their verbal fluency
    c. if each party sticks to statements of fact and refrains from stating how they feel about the other's actions
    d. if information that contradicts the other party's misperceptions is given bit by bit and not all at once

30. The "Kennedy experiment" was an application of_____ to international tension reduction.

    a. equal status contact   c. arbitration
    b. the jigsaw technique   d. the GRIT model

31. Two gas station owners in Roseville cut their gas prices in order to capture a portion of their competitor's business. However, neither gained any of the other's customers and in the long run both operated at a loss. This outcome best illustrates the dynamics of

    a. a social dilemma   c. an inequitable relationship
    b. the GRIT strategy   d. mirror-image perceptions

32. Rodney and Ralph are twin brothers who each contributed $75 to purchase a new bicycle. Rodney rides it 75 percent of the time. This would be an example of

    a. an inequitable relationship   c. a zero-sum relationship
    b. the Tragedy of the Commons   d. mirror-image perceptions

33. John believes that he is hard-working and that his wife Rachel is lazy. Rachel believes that she is hard-working and that John is lazy. This is an example of

    a. an inequitable relationship   c. a superordinate conflict
    b. mirror-image perception   d. a social trap

34. Which of the following best illustrates a superordinate goal?

    a. A college student who has been failing English gets an "A" on a paper
    b. A woman beats her husband at tennis
    c. Apartment dwellers install a television antenna they can all use
    d. An obese person loses 20 pounds in two weeks

35. According to the text, contact between two conflicting racial groups can often improve relationships and correct misperceptions. Which kind of contact is, however, least likely to have that effect?

    a. placing Black and White athletes on the same baseball team
    b. having Black and White employees work together in small groups in an industrial plant
    c. placing White policemen on duty in predominantly Black residential neighborhoods
    d. having Blacks and Whites move into the same apartment building

36. Sherif's studies of conflict in summer camp should lead one to suggest which of the following to a couple having marital difficulties?

    a. Play poker, keeping a cumulative score
    b. Encounter each other: express your true feelings
    c. Work together on something
    d. Take separate vacations

37. Factory workers want a pay rate of $18 per hour, but management offers $14 per hour. After weeks of conflict they agree to have a third party set the pay scale. After hearing both sides the third party sets the rate at $16. This is an example of resolving conflict through

    a. bargaining   c. mediation
    b. arbitration   d. conciliation

38. The GRIT model could be applied to the reduction of conflict between

    a. individuals   c. nations
    b. groups   d. all of these

39. Milton, a Jewish-American, lacks a real sense of either his Jewish or his American identity. Milton is especially likely to experience

    a. mirror-image perceptions   c. low self-esteem
    b. ingroup bias   d. the tragedy of the commons

40. Kevin and Joel, two teenage brothers, are fighting over the evening newspaper. Knowing that Kevin wants only the sports section and Joel wants only the latest stock quotations, their mother takes the paper and gives each boy the section containing the news of his interest. In this case the mother arrived at a(n)

    a. mutual compromise   c. enlightened consensus
    b. cooperative settlement   d. integrative agreement

SHORT ESSAY QUESTIONS

Answer the following questions in the space provided.

1. Define *conflict* and *peace*.

2. Describe the Tragedy of the Commons and explain its causes.

3. List three possible ways of promoting cooperation in the Prisoner's Dilemma game.

4. Briefly describe how Sherif first increased and then decreased conflict in a boys' summer camp.

5. Give the formula for an equitable relationship.

6. Under what conditions is desegregation likely to lead to improved race relations?

7. Distinguish among bargaining, mediation, and arbitration.

8. Describe the GRIT strategy for reducing conflict.

Chapter Review

1. perceived
   Peace

2. self-interests
   detriment
   Prisoner's
   Commons

3. small
   communicate
   altruistic

4. Competition
   lose

5. equity
   proportion
   compensation
   equity

6. misperceptions
   mirror-image
   confirming
   leader
   people

7. reduces
   little
   equal

8. unity
   superordinate
   cooperative

9. identities
   self-concept

10. bargain
    mediator
    lose
    win
    misperceptions
    Arbitration

11. conciliatory
    GRIT
    announces
    reciprocate
    actions
    retaliatory

Matching Terms

1. f
2. c
3. a
4. j
5. l
6. b

7. d
8. g
9. h
10. m
11. k
12. e
13. i

True-False Review

1.	F	14.	T
2.	T	15.	T
3.	F	16.	F
4.	F	17.	F
5.	F	18.	F
6.	F	19.	T
7.	T	20.	F
8.	F	21.	F
9.	T	22.	F
10.	T	23.	T
11.	F	24.	F
12.	F	25.	F
13.	T		

Multiple-Choice Practice Test

1.	a	21.	a
2.	b	22.	b
3.	d	23.	a
4.	c	24.	b
5.	a	25.	b
6.	b	26.	a
7.	a	27.	b
8.	d	28.	a
9.	d	29.	a
10.	c	30.	d
11.	a	31.	a
12.	c	32.	a
13.	b	33.	b
14.	d	34.	c
15.	a	35.	c
16.	c	36.	c
17.	a	37.	b
18.	d	38.	d
19.	b	39.	c
20.	b	40.	d

CHAPTER 14

SOCIAL PSYCHOLOGY IN THE CLINIC

CHAPTER OBJECTIVES

After completing your study of this chapter you should be able to:

1. Describe how thinking errors may contaminate the personality interpretations made by mental health professionals.

2. Describe the thought patterns of depressed persons and discuss whether their attributions are a cause or consequence of their depressed mood.

3. Describe the thought patterns associated with loneliness and social anxiety.

4. Discuss factors influencing people's reactions to illness and the role of negative emotions in health.

5. Identify social-psychological principles that can usefully be applied in treating psychological disorders.

6. Discuss the links between close relationships and well-being.

CHAPTER REVIEW

Supply the words necessary to complete each of the following statements.

1. Social psychology has contributed to improving the process of clinical
_____ and prediction, and to understanding how the ways in which we
_____ about ourselves fuel depression and anxiety. Social psychology
also examines the role of supportive relationships in health and _____.

WHAT INFLUENCES THE ACCURACY OF CLINICAL JUDGMENT?

2. Professional clinical judgment is also social judgment, subject to its principles. _____ _____ are evident when clinicians perceive expected relationships between test performances and symptoms when no relationship exists. After-the-fact psychologizing is particularly vulnerable to the _____ bias.

3. Interviewers' erroneous diagnoses of clients are often _____ since interviewers tend to seek out and recall information that _____ whatever they are looking for. The behaviors of people undergoing psychotherapy may come to fit the _____ of their therapists. Although statistical predictions may be unreliable, human _____ is even more unreliable.

4. Research on the _____ that contaminate intuitive judgments illustrates the need for rigorous _____ of intuitive conclusions.

WHAT COGNITIVE PROCESSES ACCOMPANY BEHAVIOR PROBLEMS?

5. Although depressed people are _____ thinkers, research indicates that they make surprisingly _____ judgments. Depressed people are more likely to attribute failure to causes that are _____, global, and _____.

6. Our _____ color our thinking. Depression definitely has both cognitive and _____ consequences. At the same time, evidence suggests that a pessimistic _____ style contributes to depressive reactions.

7. Those who suffer chronic _____ and states of social _____ are also caught in a vicious cycle of self-defeating social _____ and social _____. _____ is a form of social anxiety characterized by self-consciousness and worry about what others think.

8. The subfield of _____ psychology provides psychology's contribution to _____ medicine. It explores how people decide they are _____, how they explain their _____, and when they seek and follow _____. Heart disease has been linked with an _____-_____ personality. Research suggests that an attitude of _____ is good for health.

WHAT ARE SOME SOCIAL-PSYCHOLOGICAL APPROACHES TO TREATMENT?

9. In treating psychological disorders some therapists assume that internal change can be triggered by changes in _____. Experiments indicate that the things we say about ourselves can influence how we inwardly _____. This is

particularly true when we feel _____ for how we have presented ourselves.

10. A self-defeating cycle of negative attitudes and behaviors can be broken by training more _____ behavior, by positive experiences that alter _____, and by directly modifying negative _____ patterns.

11. Improved states are most likely to be maintained if people attribute their improvement to _____ factors rather than to the _____ program itself.

12. Psychologists increasingly accept the idea that social _____ is at the heart of therapy. Therapists, aided by their image as _____ communicators, aim to stimulate healthier _____ by offering cogent arguments and raising questions. The _____ route to persuasion provides the most enduring attitude and behavior change.

HOW DO SOCIAL RELATIONSHIPS SUPPORT HEALTH AND WELL-BEING?

13. Close, supportive relationships promote _____. Such relationships assist people's coping with _____, especially when they enable people to _____ their intimate emotions.

14. Close relationships also foster _____. Throughout the world, _____ people report greater happiness and are less at risk for _____.

MATCHING TERMS

Write the letter of the term on the right before the appropriate number on the left.

_____	1.	About 10 percent of men and 20 percent of women experience it.
_____	2.	A distinguishing feature of depressed persons.
_____	3.	Psychology's contribution to behavioral medicine.
_____	4.	May serve a self-handicapping function.
_____	5.	More common among adolescents than among adults.
_____	6.	Occurs when we are uncertain about our ability to impress others.
_____	7.	Integrates behavioral and medical knowledge about disease.
_____	8.	Teaches the depressed to accept credit for their successes.
_____	9.	Patients come to fit the theories of their therapists.
_____	10.	Assumes emotions will follow behavior.
_____	11.	One's habitual way of explaining life's events.
_____	12.	The study, assessment, and treatment of people with psychological difficulties.

a. clinical psychology

b. loneliness

c. major depressive episode

d. explanatory style

e. health psychology

f. alcohol abuse

g. behavioral medicine

h. sadder-but-wiser

i. self-confirming diagnosis

j. rational-emotive therapy

k. explanatory style therapy

l. social anxiety

<u>TRUE-FALSE REVIEW</u>

Circle T if the statement is true and F if it is false.

T F 1. Social psychology has contributed to the understanding but not to the treatment of psychological disorders.

T F 2. Mildly depressed people are more vulnerable to heart disease.

T F 3. In the hands of an experienced clinician, the Draw-a-Person test has very high predictive validity.

T F 4. Three out of four married people in the United States say their spouse is their best friend.

T F 5. Because of the ambiguity of their work, clinical psychologists tend to lack confidence in the accuracy of their judgments.

T F 6. In North America, young adults today are three times as likely as their grandparents were to suffer depression.

T F 7. After David Rosenhan alerted mental hospital staff members that pseudopatients might seek admission to their hospital, staff were much more accurate in recognizing real patients and those persons who were normal.

T F 8. In analyzing the childhood experiences of their clients, therapists can easily give after-the-fact interpretations that confirm their theories.

T F 9. The happiest university students are those who feel satisfied with their love life.

T F 10. The best predictor of success in graduate school is provided by the assessment of a trained interviewer.

T F 11. Close relationships promote psychological but not physical health.

T F 12. Research has indicated that depressed persons may be more accurate than nondepressives are in estimating their degree of control over the environment.

T F 13. The most recent analyses of psychotherapeutic influence focus on how therapists establish credibility.

T F 14. Adolescents are more likely than adults to report feeling lonely.

T F 15. Males and females feel lonely under somewhat different conditions.

T F 16. Women's physical and mental skills fluctuate noticeably with their menstrual cycles.

T F 17. Alcohol abuse sometimes serves a self-handicapping function.

T F 18. Healthy behaviors are an essential contributor to the longevity of many optimists.

T F 19. Rates of suicide and depression are higher among unmarried people.

T F 20. Explanatory style therapy attempts to alleviate depression by teaching victims to accept credit for their successes and to recognize how circumstances can make things go wrong.

T F 21. Intuitive or clinical predictions tend to be more reliable than statistical predictions.

T F 22. Depressed people are more likely than nondepressed people to blame themselves for their own failures.

T F 23. Depression is both a cause and a consequence of negative cognitions.

T F 24. Lonely people seem to have more negative perceptions of others.

T F 25. An increasing number of psychologists believe that social influence is at the heart of psychotherapy.

MULTIPLE-CHOICE PRACTICE TEST

Circle the correct letter.

1. According to the text, social psychology has contributed to the following achievements <u>except</u>

    a. our understanding of psychological disorders
    b. the treatment of psychological disorders
    c. improving the process of clinical judgment and prediction
    d. the definition of psychological disorder

2. The text suggests that clinicians may continue to have confidence in uninformative or ambiguous tests because of human susceptibility to

    a. the inoculation effect   c. the representativeness heuristic
    b. learned helplessness   d   illusory correlation

3. After complaining of hearing voices, David Rosenhan and his associates were diagnosed as schizophrenic and hospitalized. Clinicians' subsequent attempts to explain the diagnosis demonstrated

   a. the bias in after-the-fact explanations
   b. the fundamental attribution error
   c. their susceptibility to the just world phenomenon
   d. the benefits of clinical intuition

4. Research on the relationship between marriage and happiness indicates that

   a. married men but not married women are happier than their single counterparts
   b. people who say their marriage is satisfying rarely report being unhappy or depressed
   c. about one-third of married Americans say their marriage is "very happy"
   d. happiness seems to promote marriage but marriage does not promote happiness

5. When people are asked, "What is necessary for your happiness?" most mention
   _____ first.

   a. meaningful work   c. close personal relationships
   b. money   d. good physical and mental health

6. According to the text, which of the following statements is accurate?

   a. Social psychologists are more susceptible to illusory thinking than are clinical psychologists
   b. Projective tests actually give more useful information than do objective tests
   c. People who come for therapy want to hear negative things about themselves
   d. Behaviors of people undergoing psychotherapy come to fit the theories of their therapists

7. Research evidence suggests that professional clinicians

   a. are relatively immune to the illusion of control
   b. should rely more heavily on clinical intuition than on statistical prediction
   c. are too readily convinced of their own after-the-fact analyses
   d. are less susceptible to illusory thinking than are research psychologists

8. Compared with college women who have experienced nonsexual traumas, sexually abused women reported more health problems especially if

   a. they had kept their secret to themselves
   b. the abuser was a relative
   c. they were high in self-monitoring
   d. they were planning to marry in the next year

9. According to the text, which of the following helps explain the correlation between intelligence and health?

   a. depression
   b. loneliness
   c. poverty
   d. alcohol abuse

10. Which of the following attributions regarding a failure or setback illustrates the stable quality of a depressed person's explanatory style?

    a. "It's all my fault."
    b. "It's going to last forever."
    c. "The whole world is against me."
    d. "It's going to affect everything I do."

11. Studies of depression challenge the common presumption that

    a. depressed people are negative thinkers
    b. more women than men suffer major depressive episodes
    c. depressed people are unrealistic
    d. a depressed mood has both cognitive and behavioral consequences

12. Research on loneliness indicates that

    a. adults are more likely than adolescents to report feeling lonely
    b. lonely people are more realistic than those who do not report feelings of loneliness
    c. loneliness coincides with aloneness
    d. lonely people tend to perceive others in negative ways

13. When researchers had relatively depressed and nondepressed college students observe whether their pressing a button was linked to a light turning on, the results indicated that the

    a. depressed students underestimated their degree of control
    b. depressed students were quite accurate in estimating their degree of control
    c. nondepressed students were quite accurate in estimating their degree of control
    d. nondepressed students underestimated their degree of control

14. Among U.S. residents, women _____ than men.

    a. have higher rates of cancer
    b. use fewer prescription drugs
    c. visit physicians more frequently
    d. report fewer symptoms of illness

15. Research on the social thinking of people vulnerable to depression indicates that

    a. depression is both a cause and a consequence of their negative thinking
    b. they have surprisingly positive self-concepts
    c. males and females who are depressed think very differently
    d. they are more vulnerable to both illusory correlation and the fundamental attribution error

16. Compared to nondepressed people, depressed people are more likely to attribute their failures and setbacks to causes that are

    a. unstable   c. internal
    b. specific   d. situational

17. According to Martin Seligman, the decline of religion and family and the growth of the "you can do it" idea have contributed to a large increase in

    a. character disorders   c. phobias
    b. schizophrenia   d. depression

18. Research indicates that heart disease is most clearly linked with an _____ personality.

    a. introverted   c. anger-prone
    b. apathetic   d. assertive

19. Members of baseball's Hall of Fame who offered pessimistic explanations for bad events such as losing big games

    a. died at younger ages
    b. were more susceptible to loneliness
    c. were less successful in life after retiring from baseball
    d. were more likely to be divorced

20. Satisfaction with _____ seems to be the best predictor of overall happiness.

    a   job   c. finances
    b. marriage   d. community

21. Research suggests that an attitude of _____ is generally good for health.

    a. competitiveness   c. skepticism
    b. optimism   d. humility

22. In contrast to those who are not lonely, lonely people tend to

    a. spend more time talking about themselves when conversing with a stranger
    b. be more inclined to blame others for their problems
    c. be more susceptible to the illusion of control
    d. be more inclined to idealize members of the opposite sex

23. Brodt and Zimbardo found that shy women were no longer shy when they

    a. were provided an alternative explanation for their social anxiety
    b. were provided alcohol before interacting with others
    c. discovered most people feel shy
    d. were taught to blame their failures on circumstances beyond their control

24. Students who had been induced to write self-laudatory essays

    a. expressed higher self-esteem in private self-ratings
    b. were more likely to make the fundamental attribution error
    c. showed greater hostility to a stranger
    d. were more likely to rationalize their failure to help a person in need

25. Which of the following is not an example of a therapy that utilizes the "attitudes-follow-behavior" principle?

    a. assertiveness training   c. self-help groups
    b. rational-emotive therapy   d. psychoanalysis

26. Research suggests that optimists

    a. recover more slowly from coronary bypass surgery
    b. tend to offer stable, global, and internal explanations for bad events
    c. may see themselves as invulnerable and thus fail to take sensible precautions
    d. are less susceptible to depression but more susceptible to anxiety

27. Explanatory style therapy attempts to teach depressed people to

    a. accept credit for their successes and to note how circumstances make things go wrong
    b. avoid the fundamental attribution error
    c. attribute their depression to their own personality traits
    d. focus on others rather than on themselves

28. Graduates of a weight-control program were more successful in maintaining their weight loss if they had been

    a. led to credit their changed eating behavior to their own effort
    b. punished for violating rules of the treatment program
    c. promised large rewards for successfully losing weight
    d. led to credit their changed eating behavior to the therapist

29. A meta-analysis of 134 studies that involved the prediction of human behavior or the making of psychological or medical diagnoses and prognoses revealed that

    a. in the vast majority of studies clinical intuition surpassed statistical prediction
    b. in the vast majority of studies statistical prediction surpassed clinical intuition
    c. the use of first hand interviews typically surpassed both statistical and clinical prediction
    d. a combination of statistical methods and clinical intuition produced the most accurate prediction

30. Rats injected with live cancer cells were more likely to die of tumors if they also received
    _____.

    a. escapable shock   c. a high-fat diet
    b. inescapable shock   d. moderate doses of radiation

31. What error in thinking may contribute to a person's feeling of guilt after a close relative commits suicide?

    a. self-serving bias   c. the fundamental attribution error
    b. hindsight bias   d. depressive realism

32. The epidemic that suddenly affected Santa Monica students during a musical performance best illustrated the effect of

    a. perceived control on reactions to stress
    b. conditioning on the suppression of the immune system
    c. social influence on the interpretation of symptoms
    d. pessimism on physical health

33. Studies on people's reactions to their own physical condition indicate that

    a. half or more of all heart attack victims die before seeking or receiving medical help
    b. college students tend to overreport medical complaints
    c. women's mental skills fluctuate noticeably with their menstrual cycle
    d. most people are good at estimating their blood pressure

34. Chronically lonely people tend to blame _____ for their poor social relationships.

    a. their parents or early childhood experiences
    b. themselves
    c. the uncaring attitudes of the people around them
    d. cultural values and patterns

35. Dr. Jones is a psychologist who specializes in the causes and control of stress. Dr. Jones is most likely a(n) _____ psychologist.

    a. consumer   c. forensic
    b. educational   d. health

36. Miguel suffers from chronic depression. How is he likely to respond when told that he failed the test to renew his driver's license?

    a. "Yesterday was just my unlucky day."
    b. "I imagine very few people have passed that same test."
    c. "The person giving the test is incompetent."
    d. "I am a poor driver and always will be."

37. Mary wants advice on how to cope with the stress of a new job. She would be best advised to approach her new job with a sense of

    a. skepticism and humility
    b. ambition and competitiveness
    c. urgency and time-consciousness
    d. control and optimism

38. As a result of participating in a program to help him quit smoking, Bill has not had a cigarette for three weeks. He is least likely to return to smoking if he attributes his success in quitting the habit to

    a. his own motivation
    b. the therapist who helped him quit
    c. the support of his friends
    d. the unique nature of the therapeutic program

39. Yolanda is a mildly depressed college student. According to the text, she

    a. probably suffers from the better-than-average phenomenon
    b. assumes that her behavior is well-accepted by others
    c. demonstrates the sadder-but-wiser effect
    d. is below average in intelligence

40. Gayle, a Freudian analyst, finds that, without exception, her patients report dreams closely related to their emotional problems and that these dreams are easily understood in terms of Freud's theory of personality. According to the text, which statement may best explain why the dreams and the problems of Gayle's patients are so consistent with Freudian theory?

    a. Freud's theory is the oldest and most comprehensive of all the theories of personality
    b. Freud's theory is more ambiguous than any other theory, and thus any problem fits into its framework
    c. The patients are perhaps induced to give information that is consistent with Gayle's theoretical orientation
    d. Freudian psychotherapists are "true believers" and Gayle's report is an attempt to convert other therapists to her orientation

SHORT ESSAY QUESTIONS

Answer the following questions in the space provided.

1. Explain how each of the following phenomena may characterize the judgments of mental health professionals:

    A. illusory correlation

    B. hindsight bias

    C. self-fulfilling prophecy

2. Describe the thought patterns of depressed people. Is their attributional style the cause or the consequence of their depressed mood?

3. Describe the thought patterns associated with loneliness and social anxiety.

4. Describe how our emotions can influence our health.

5. Identify three social-psychological principles that can be applied in the treatment of psychological disorders.

6. Briefly describe how social relations can influence health and happiness.

Chapter Review

1. judgment
   think
   happiness

2. Illusory
   correlations
   hindsight

3. self-confirming
   verifies
   theories
   intuition

4. errors
   testing

5. negative
   accurate
   stable
   internal

6. moods
   behavioral
   explanatory

7. loneliness
   anxiety
   cognitions
   behaviors
   Shyness

8. health
   behavioral
   ill
   symptoms
   treatment
   anger-prone
   optimism

9. behavior
   feel
   responsible

10. skillful
    self-perceptions
    thought

11. internal
    treatment

12. influence
    credible
    thinking
    central

13. health
    stress
    confide

14. happiness
    married
    depression

Matching Terms

1. c
2. h
3. e
4. f
5. b
6. l

7. g
8. k
9. i
10. j
11. d
12. a

True-False Review

1.	F	14.	T
2.	T	15.	T
3.	F	16.	F
4.	T	17.	T
5.	F	18.	T
6.	T	19.	T
7.	F	20.	T
8.	T	21.	F
9.	T	22.	T
10.	F	23.	T
11.	F	24.	T
12.	T	25.	T
13.	F		

Multiple-Choice Practice Test

1.	d	21.	b
2.	d	22.	a
3.	a	23.	a
4.	b	24.	a
5.	c	25.	d
6.	d	26.	c
7.	c	27.	a
8.	a	28.	a
9.	c	29.	b
10.	b	30.	b
11.	c	31.	b
12.	d	32.	c
13.	b	33.	a
14.	c	34.	b
15.	a	35.	d
16.	c	36.	d
17.	d	37.	d
18.	c	38.	a
19.	a	39.	c
20.	b	40.	c

CHAPTER 15

SOCIAL PSYCHOLOGY IN COURT

CHAPTER OBJECTIVES

After completing your study of this chapter you should be able to:

1. Identify issues pertinent to both social psychology and the law.

2. Discuss findings on eyewitness testimony and describe ways of reducing error.

3. Identify defendant characteristics that may influence jurors' judgments, and describe the effects of the judge's instructions.

4. Show how jurors' individual dispositions may influence their verdicts.

5. Discuss how a jury functions as a group.

6. Explain the value of simulated juries.

CHAPTER REVIEW

Supply the words necessary to complete each of the following statements.

1. We can think of the _____ as a miniature social world, one that magnifies everyday social processes with major consequences for those involved.

HOW RELIABLE IS EYEWITNESS TESTIMONY?

2. Experiments suggest that jurors find eyewitnesses _____, sometimes even eyewitnesses whose testimony is _____. Eyewitnesses' certainty about their judgments often relates only modestly to their _____.

3. Errors creep in because we construct our _____ based partly on what we perceived at the time and partly on our expectations and beliefs. _____ what happened commits people to their recollections, whether

accurate or not. In addition, people tend to adjust what they say to _____ their listeners and then come to _____ their altered message. Receiving confirming _____ increases eyewitnesses' confidence in their judgments.

4. To increase the accuracy of eyewitnesses and jurors, experts suggest that we _____ police interviewers, minimize _____ lineup identifications, and educate jurors about _____ testimony.

WHAT OTHER FACTORS INFLUENCE JUROR JUDGMENTS?

5. The evidence usually is clear enough that jurors can set aside their _____. But when the evidence is ambiguous, jurors may feel sympathetic to a defendant who is _____ or who is _____ to them. When jurors focus attention on the _____, their biases seem to have minimal effect.

6. Jurors have difficulty following the judge's instructions to ignore _____ publicity or _____ evidence. One experiment found that a judge's order to ignore testimony _____ to the testimony's impact.

7. _____ people about the inadmissibility of various types of evidence diminishes its impact. _____ witnesses' testimony and removing objectionable material provides another way of eliminating inadmissible testimony.

WHAT INFLUENCES THE INDIVIDUAL JUROR?

8. In making decisions, jurors construct a story that makes sense of all the _____ and consider the judge's _____ concerning the available verdict categories. A major concern is the jurors' ability to understand _____ information. Despite the concern about scientific jury _____, research indicates that _____ is a more potent determinant of jurors' verdicts than their personal characteristics.

9. In a _____ case, the jurors' characteristics can influence their verdicts. For example, jurors who favor the _____ penalty appear more likely to vote to convict certain types of defendants. They also tend to be more _____, that is, rigid, punitive, and contemptuous of those with lower social status.

HOW DO GROUP INFLUENCES AFFECT JURORS?

10. The chances are about two in _____ that jurors will initially not agree on a verdict. Yet after discussion, _____ percent of juries reach a consensus.

11. The jury's verdict is usually the alternative favored by at least _____ of the jurors at the outset. Without such a majority, a _____ jury is likely to result.

12. Jurors in the minority are likely to be most persuasive when they are_____, persistent, and self-confident, especially if they begin to trigger _____ from the majority.

13. The finding that group deliberation leads high authoritarians to recommend _____ punishment and low authoritarians to recommend more _____ punishment suggests that group _____ can occur in juries.

14. When evidence is not highly incriminating, juries tend to become _____ lenient after deliberating. A minority that favors acquittal has a _____ chance than one that favors conviction. To the extent that _____ influence moves jurors, we can hope that a jury's collective judgment will be superior to that of its average member.

15. Recent research raises questions about the wisdom of several Supreme Court decisions permitting _____ juries and juries not required to reach _____ verdicts. Compared to smaller juries, larger juries are more likely to contain members of _____ groups and to recall trial testimony more _____.

16. We must be careful in _____ research findings to actual courtrooms. Laboratory jury _____ help us to formulate theories that we can use to _____ the more complex world of everyday life.

MATCHING TERMS

Write the letter of the term on the right before the appropriate number on the left.

_____	1. Low authoritarians become more lenient, high authoritarians become more punitive.
_____	2. Provides a way of eliminating inadmissible evidence.
_____	3. Help researchers to formulate theories that can be used to interpret the complex world.
_____	4. Persuasive but not always accurate.
_____	5. May elicit reactance.
_____	6. Used by lawyers to stack juries in their favor.
_____	7. More concerned with crime control than with due process of law.
_____	8. Without it a hung jury is likely.
_____	9. Benefits the defendant.
_____	10. Jurors' personal biases are more likely to influence the verdict.
_____	11. Favoring acquittal, it stands a better chance.
_____	12. Remembering wrong information.

a. misinformation effect

b. physical attractiveness

c. death-qualified jurors

d. judges' instructions

e. ambiguous cases

f. simulated juries

g. two-thirds majority

h. minority influence

i. group polarization

j. jury selection

k. videotaping

l. eyewitness testimony

Circle T if the statement is true and F if it is false.

T F   1. According to the text, social psychologists have conducted experiments on the courtroom because it provides an excellent context for studying the effect of the physical environment on behavior.

T F   2. The U.S. Supreme Court has declared that one factor to be considered in judging eyewitness accuracy is the level of certainty demonstrated by the witness.

T F   3. Eyewitnesses who are shown to have poor eyesight may still have an impact on jurors' judgments.

T F   4. Eyewitnesses' certainty about their own accuracy in viewing a crime is closely related to their actual accuracy.

T F   5. After suggestive questioning, witnesses may believe that a red light was actually green.

T F   6. The more we retell a story, the more we may convince ourselves of a falsehood.

T F   7. To increase eyewitness accuracy, interviewers should begin by allowing eyewitnesses to offer their own unprompted recollections.

T F   8. Live and videotaped testimony have much the same impact on jurors.

T F   9. Attractive defendants are treated more severely than are unattractive defendants.

T F 10. Most jurors, when asked by a judge to "raise your hand if you've read anything about this case that would prejudice you," acknowledge their preconceptions.

T F 11. A person accused of a politically motivated burglary is judged less guilty if his political views are similar to those of the jurors.

T F 12. Simulated juries cannot provide helpful insights into the dynamics of actual courtrooms.

T F 13. When the evidence is clear and jurors focus on it, their biases seem to have minimal effect on their judgments.

T F 14. The U.S. Supreme Court has ruled that "death-qualified" jurors constitute a biased sample.

T F 15. False lineup identifications are reduced when witnesses simply make yes/no judgments in response to a sequence of people.

T F 16. The U.S. Supreme Court has disallowed five-member juries.

T F 17. When the evidence is not highly incriminating, jurors tend to become more lenient after deliberating.

T F 18. Hung juries occur in about 20 percent of all jury trials.

T F 19. People who favor the death penalty are also more prone to vote a defendant guilty.

T F 20. Research indicates that U.S. federal judges have sentenced Blacks to longer prison terms than Whites.

T F 21. One study of criminal and civil cases found that four times in five the judge concurred with the jury's decision.

T F 22. Smaller juries may be less likely to embody a community's diversity.

T F 23. Research indicates that 12-person juries are twice as likely as 6-person juries to have hung verdicts.

T F 24. Juries are more persuaded by evidence when it is presented in the order of a narrative story.

T F 25. Homicide rates have risen when states have abandoned the death penalty.

MULTIPLE-CHOICE PRACTICE TEST

Circle the correct letter.

1. According to the text, which of the following statements regarding social psychology and the courtroom is true?

   a. Most of the government research funds available to social psychologists have been designated for the study of courtroom procedures
   b. The courtroom is a miniature social world, one that magnifies everyday social processes with major consequences for those involved
   c. The study of criminal cases can provide important new insight into the causes of aggression and conflict
   d. Social psychology had its roots in the study of the courtroom

2. Jurors who were asked to observe and evaluate eyewitnesses to the staged theft of a University of Alberta calculator

    a. believed both correct and incorrect eyewitnesses most of the time
    b. were suspicious of both correct and incorrect eyewitnesses
    c. believed the correct eyewitnesses but were suspicious of the incorrect eyewitnesses
    d. were suspicious of incorrect female eyewitnesses but tended to believe incorrect male eyewitnesses

3. Research suggests that, in comparison to eyewitnesses who cannot recall the trivial details surrounding a crime, those eyewitnesses who correctly remember trivial details

    a. have a better memory for the culprit's face
    b. have a poorer memory for the culprit's face
    c. are less susceptible to misleading questions
    d. are more susceptible to misleading questions

4. Studies of the impact of eyewitness testimony indicate that

    a. eyewitnesses who have been discredited have no influence on a jury's judgments
    b. when witnessing conditions are shown to have been poor, jurors do not believe the eyewitness testimony
    c. eyewitnesses who are shown to have poor eyesight have no effect on the jurors' judgments
    d. None of these is true

5. Research has indicated that false lineup identifications can be reduced by

    a. having witnesses make individual yes/no judgments in response to a sequence of people
    b. reminding witnesses that the offender may not be in the lineup
    c. using a "blank" lineup that contains no suspects and screening out those who make false identifications
    d. All of these

6. Which of the following is not part of the literature discussed in the text on social psychology and the courtroom?

    a. how the defendant's characteristics can influence jurors' judgments
    b. how the jurors' own characteristics can influence their judgments
    c. how the physical environment of the jury room influences jurors' judgments
    d. how the judge's instructions influence jurors' judgments

7. In comparison to those who did not receive confirming feedback on their testimony, eyewitnesses who received confirming feedback

   a. often felt manipulated and were less confident about their judgment
   b. recalled being more confident when making their initial judgment
   c. reported that the feedback significantly increased their confidence from when they made their initial judgment
   d. expressed greater liking for the experimenter and willingness to participate in additional research

8. When students were presented with a hypothetical robbery-murder with circumstantial evidence but no eyewitness testimony, only 18 percent voted for conviction. With the addition of eyewitness testimony to the circumstantial evidence,

   a. the majority of students voted for conviction provided the eyesight of the eyewitness was not called into question
   b. the majority of students voted for conviction even if the eyesight of the eyewitness was called into question
   c. 35 percent of the students voted for conviction provided the vision of the eyewitness was not called into question
   d. even fewer students voted for conviction if the eyesight of the witness was shown to be very poor

9. Students at California State University, Hayward, witnessed an assault on a professor. Seven weeks later when asked to identify the assailant from a group of six photographs,

   a. the majority made a wrong identification
   b. the majority chose the right person but distorted important details of the assault
   c. the majority of females chose the right person but the majority of males identified the wrong person
   d. upperclassmen were more accurate than freshmen in identifying the assailant

10. Research on memory construction indicates that suggestive questioning can lead people to believe that

   a. a yield sign was actually a stop sign
   b. a red light was actually green
   c. a robber had a moustache when he did not
   d. all of these

11. Research indicates that having eyewitnesses rehearse their answers to questions before taking the witness stand

    a. raises uncertainty in the minds of eyewitnesses as to what they actually saw
    b. increases their confidence about what they saw
    c. increases their confidence but also heightens their anxiety about appearing in court
    d. invariably leads them to give a much more detailed and accurate account of what they saw

12. When experts provide jurors information on the conditions under which eyewitness accounts <u>are</u> trustworthy

    a. jurors become more discerning
    b. jurors demonstrate reactance and are even more likely to accept inaccurate testimony
    c. jurors are not influenced by the information experts provide
    d. less intelligent jurors demonstrate reactance but more intelligent jurors analyze eyewitness testimony more carefully

13. Research comparing juries' decisions with those made by a judge has indicated that

    a. when a judge disagrees with the jury's decision it is usually because the jury convicts someone the judge would acquit
    b. juries generally recommend longer prison terms than judges are inclined to give
    c. two-thirds of the time the jury and the judge disagree
    d. four times in five the judge concurs with the jury's decision

14. Research has indicated that, compared to less attractive defendants, physically attractive defendants are

    a. less likely to be found guilty and if found guilty receive less punishment
    b. less likely to be found guilty but if found guilty receive more punishment
    c. more likely to be found guilty and if found guilty receive more punishment
    d. more likely to be found guilty but if found guilty receive less punishment

15. According to the text, a jury may demonstrate reactance in response to a

    a. dogmatic prosecuting attorney
    b. judge's instructions to ignore testimony
    c. self-confident eyewitness
    d. timid defense attorney

16. Videotaped testimony

    a. allows the court to edit out inadmissible evidence
    b. has been disallowed by the U.S. Supreme Court in real trials
    c. does not have the same impact as live testimony
    d. All of these are true

17. In studying the impact of statistical information on jurors' judgments, Gary Wells and his colleagues conclude that

    a. when people <u>understand</u> the high statistical probabilities of someone having committed a crime, they are persuaded of a defendant's guilt
    b. even when people understand statistical probabilities, to be persuaded of a defendant's guilt, they need the numbers to be supported by a convincing story
    c. in comparison to laypeople, experienced trial judges show both a clearer understanding of statistical probabilities and the ability to apply that information appropriately
    d. statistical information is even more persuasive than is eyewitness testimony in shaping juries' verdicts

18. A judge's instructions to jurors that they ignore inadmissible evidence are most likely to be followed if given

    a. immediately after the inadmissible evidence has been presented
    b. as a forewarning before the evidence is presented
    c. just before the jury retires to deliberate on the evidence
    d. after the prosecution has presented its case but before the defense calls its witnesses

19. Survey researchers sometimes assist defense attorneys by using "scientific jury selection" to eliminate potential jurors likely to be unsympathetic. Results indicated that in the first nine important trials in which the defense relied on such methods, it

    a. won all nine
    b. won two
    c. won seven
    d. lost all nine

20. In 1986, the U.S. Supreme Court in a split decision

    a. ruled that death-qualified jurors are a biased sample
    b. overturned a lower court ruling that death-qualified jurors are a biased sample
    c. ruled that Georgia's five-member juries were as reliable and accurate as twelve-member juries
    d. overturned a lower court decision that six-member juries could decide cases involving the death penalty

21. People who do not oppose the death penalty are

    a. likely to have been involved in some crime themselves
    b. more likely to favor the prosecution
    c. likely to have deep religious convictions
    d. likely to be middle-aged or elderly

22. Jurors who are more prone to vote guilty tend to be

    a. more authoritarian
    b. lower in self-esteem
    c. from the upper socioeconomic class
    d. higher in self-efficacy

23. Research on the individual characteristics of jurors, such as personality and general attitudes, indicates that

    a. these characteristics are as important as the evidence itself in determining jurors' verdicts
    b. these characteristics have their strongest effect when the evidence is ambiguous
    c. males are less likely to find a defendant guilty than are females
    d. highly religious persons are less likely to find a defendant guilty than are less religious persons

24. Someone accused of a crime is judged more sympathetically

    a. by females than by males
    b. if he or she appears to have personality characteristics that are complementary to the one who judges
    c. if he or she appears similar to the one who judges
    d. if there was a bystander who watched and did not intervene

25. Which of the following statements regarding the influence of minorities in jury deliberations is true?

    a. Minorities composed of women are more influential than minorities composed of men
    b. Frequently a minority view prevails and causes the majority to reverse its verdict
    c. A minority that favors acquittal stands a better chance of influencing the majority than does a minority that favors conviction
    d. Minorities composed of high authoritarians are more influential than minorities composed of low authoritarians

26. What is meant by the "two-thirds-majority" scheme?

    a. Two-thirds of all people asked refuse to serve on a jury
    b. Two out of three times judges agree with the jury's decision
    c. A two-thirds majority is a better rule than consensus for a jury to follow in reaching a verdict
    d. The jury verdict is usually the alternative favored by at least two-thirds of the jurors at the outset

27. The fact that high authoritarians who initially recommended strong punishments were even more punitive after group deliberation suggests that _____ can occur in juries.

    a. group polarization   c. groupthink
    b. social facilitation   d. reactance

28. Dunning and Perretta reported that eyewitnesses who made their identifications in less than 10 to 12 seconds were about _____ percent accurate.

    a. 30   c. 50
    b. 70   d. 90

29. From research on minority influence we can speculate that jurors in the minority

    a. will never have a significant effect on the majority
    b. can be persuasive if they state their case tentatively
    c. can be persuasive if they are consistent and self-confident
    d. can be persuasive if they are females

30. Survey research findings report that _____ juries ultimately reach the verdict favored by the majority on the first ballot.

    a. 9 out of 10   c. 5 out of 10
    b. 7 out of 10   d. 3 out of 10

31. In terms of the number of people who deliberate, jury research suggests that

    a. Six heads are better than twelve
    b. Twelve heads are better than one
    c. Six males are better than nine females
    d. One head is better than twelve

32. What criticism has been made of the use of six-member juries instead of twelve-member juries?

    a. six-member juries are less likely to take their task seriously
    b. six-member juries are less likely to embody a community's diversity
    c. six-member juries are more likely to be hung juries
    d. six-member juries are more likely to become dominated by an authoritarian individual

33. Studies comparing twelve-member juries with six-member juries indicate that

    a. twelve-member juries are likely to elicit more balanced participation per juror than are six-member juries
    b. twelve-member juries are twice as likely as six-member juries are to have hung verdicts
    c. six-member juries tend to take their task more seriously than twelve-member juries do
    d. twelve-member juries are significantly more likely to convict a defendant than are six-member juries

34. According to the text, simulated juries

    a. can help us formulate theories we can use to interpret the more complex world
    b. are almost identical to real juries so that we can readily generalize from one to the other
    c. have been viewed by the majority of Supreme Court judges as valuable in predicting the behavior of actual juries
    d. have mundane but not experimental realism

35. Whose eyewitness testimony is probably the most reliable?

    a. Thressa's report immediately after a bank robbery. She was simply asked by police to tell in her own words what happened.
    b. Sheryl's testimony about a grocery store hold-up. She has been interviewed eight times by the prosecuting attorney before appearing in court.
    c. David's testimony about a car accident. He has been interviewed three times by the defense attorney before his court appearance.
    d. Susan's report immediately after observing an attempted rape. She was asked very specific questions by the police, who believed they already had a suspect in custody.

36. Attorney Johnson will be defending James S., who is accused of raping a 22-year-old woman. Who of the following jurors is likely to be least sympathetic to his client's case?

    a. John, a 40-year-old plumber who once served a sentence for burglary
    b. Todd, a 22-year-old college student who is a political liberal
    c. Wilma, a 42-year-old mother of two who tends to be authoritarian
    d. Rita, a 32-year-old television executive who opposes the death penalty

37. Attorney Miller is defending Mary, a 20-year-old college student, who is being tried for failing to pay income tax. What should she do to boost Mary's chances of being acquitted?

a. Select Bill and Philip who are also college students to serve as jurors
b. Have Mary appear in court as attractively dressed as possible
c. Select jurors who oppose the death penalty
d. She should do all of these things

38. You have just been appointed to serve as a new county judge. You are concerned about the effect inadmissible evidence may have on the jury in an upcoming trial of a case involving rape. You anticipate that the defense attorney will seek to introduce evidence regarding the victim's prior sexual history. To minimize the impact of such evidence on the jury, you should

a. say nothing about such inadmissible evidence to the jury
b. remind the jury before the trial that the victim's previous sexual history is irrelevant
c. tell the jury that the evidence is inadmissible only after the defense attempts to introduce it
d. ask the defendant to refute any damaging evidence about her previous sexual history

39. A twelve-member jury has heard all the evidence in a child abuse case and is beginning to deliberate. At the outset five favor acquittal of the defendant and seven favor conviction. The jury will probably

a. be unable to reach a verdict and be a hung jury
b. bring in a guilty verdict
c. vote for acquittal
d. vote for acquittal if the defendant is female and for conviction if the defendant is male

40. After hearing evidence in a murder trial, twelve jurors tend to believe the evidence is insufficient to convict the 25-year-old Black defendant. According to the group polarization hypothesis, after the jurors deliberate

a. they will be more convinced the defendant is guilty
b. they will be more convinced the evidence is insufficient to convict
c. they will be evenly split with some convinced he is guilty and others convinced he is innocent
d. they will be split with a minority favoring acquittal and the majority favoring conviction

<u>SHORT ESSAY QUESTIONS</u>

Answer the following questions in the space provided.

1. Briefly explain how error may creep into eyewitness testimony.

2. Explain how error in eyewitness testimony might be reduced.

3. Identify two defendant characteristics that may influence jurors' judgments.

4. What strategies can be used to minimize, or even eliminate, the effect of inadmissible evidence on jurors' judgments?

5. What does research indicate regarding the effects of jurors' own characteristics on their verdicts?

6. Briefly give two examples of how juries are swayed by the same influences that impact other types of groups.

7. Discuss the value of simulated juries as well as their possible limitations.

ANSWER KEY

Chapter Review

1. courtroom

2. persuasive
   inaccurate
   accuracy

3. memories
   Retelling
   please
   believe
   feedback

4. train
   false
   eyewitness

5. biases
   attractive
   similar
   evidence

6. pretrial
   inadmissible
   added

7. Forewarning
   Videotaping

8. evidence
   instructions
   statistical
   selection
   evidence

9. close
   death
   authoritarian

10. three
    95

11. two-thirds
    hung

12. consistent
    defections

13. stronger
    lenient
    polarization

14. more
    better
    informational

15. six-person
    unanimous
    minority
    accurately

16. generalizing
    experiments
    interpret

Matching Terms

1. i
2. k
3. f
4. l
5. d
6. j
7. c
8. g
9. b
10. e
11. h
12. a

True-False Review

1.	F	14.	F
2.	T	15.	T
3.	T	16.	T
4.	F	17.	T
5.	T	18.	F
6.	T	19.	T
7.	T	20.	T
8.	T	21.	T
9.	F	22.	T
10.	F	23.	T
11.	T	24.	T
12.	F	25.	F
13.	T		

Multiple-Choice Practice Test

1.	b	21.	b
2.	a	22.	a
3.	b	23.	b
4.	d	24.	c
5.	d	25.	c
6.	c	26.	d
7.	b	27.	a
8.	b	28.	d
9.	a	29.	c
10.	d	30.	a
11.	b	31.	b
12.	a	32.	b
13.	d	33.	b
14.	a	34.	a
15.	b	35.	a
16.	a	36.	c
17.	b	37.	d
18.	b	38.	b
19.	c	39.	a
20.	b	40.	b

CHAPTER 16

SOCIAL PSYCHOLOGY AND THE SUSTAINABLE FUTURE

CHAPTER OBJECTIVES

After completing your study of this chapter you should be able to:

1. Discuss the nature of the global crisis.

2. Identify two different routes to sustainable lifestyles.

3. Describe the relationship between materialism and well-being.

4. Discuss how our capacity for adaptation and tendency to make social comparisons explain the psychology of consumption.

5. Explain psychology's potential contributions to a sustainable future.

CHAPTER REVIEW

Supply the words necessary to complete each of the following statements.

AN ENVIRONMENTAL CALL TO ACTION

1. For many people on earth these are, materially, the _____ of times. However, increasing _____ and increasing _____ have combined to overshoot the earth's carrying capacity. These increases have produced the serious problems of _____, global _____, and environmental _____.

ENABLING SUSTAINABLE LIVING

2. One route to a sustainable future is through increasing technological _____ and agricultural productivity. A second route is through decreasing population and controlling _____. For example, one proposal is to tax people on the basis of what they _____ rather than on the

265

basis of what they _____. Public policy could also give business and industry more _____ for conserving and more _____ for consuming.

THE SOCIAL PSYCHOLOGY OF MATERIALISM AND WEALTH

3. In the 1970s and 1980s materialism _____, most clearly in the United States. New American collegians now rank becoming "very well-off financially" as their _____ objective. Although there is some correlation between national wealth and _____, once nations reach about $10,000 GNP per person, higher levels of national wealth are not predictive of increased _____. Similarly, once basic needs are met within a country, the correlation between income and personal happiness is _____. Compared to 1957, today's Americans are twice as _____ and _____ happier.

4. Those who strive most for _____ tend to live with lower well-being. Students identify self-esteem, _____, and autonomy as the emotional needs that are met by personally satisfying events.

5. The _____-level phenomenon is our tendency to adapt to a given level of _____ and react to changes from that level.

6. Much of life revolves around social _____. Feeding our luxury fever is our tendency to compare _____.

7. Adaptation can also enable us to adjust _____. Experiments that lower our _____ standards can renew contentment.

8. Psychology's studies of the good life point to the importance of _____ relationships and faith _____. In addition, positive _____ habits, and the experience of _____, in which we lose consciousness of self and time, enhance life quality.

MATCHING TERMS

Write the letter of the term on the right before the appropriate number on the left.

_____	1. So absorbed in an activity we lose consciousness of self and time.
_____	2. New collegians rank this as their most important objective.
_____	3. Imaginative exercises in deprivation can trigger this.
_____	4. Only 28 percent of Americans worry a great deal about this.
_____	5. Difficulty predicting the intensity and duration of our future emotions.
_____	6. One route to sustainable lifestyles.
_____	7. Elements of a genuinely good life.
_____	8. Soaring wealth and greater depression.
_____	9. Our feelings of satisfaction and dissatisfaction are relative to our prior achievements.

a. adaptation-level phenomenon

b. technological efficiency

c. the American paradox

d. flow

e. impact bias

f. being very well off financially

g. downward social comparisons

h. global warming

i. close relationships, faith communities, engaging activity

TRUE-FALSE REVIEW

Circle T if the statement is true and F if it is false.

T F 1. Strong evidence for global warming does not yet exist.

T F 2. The five warmest years on record have occurred since 1998.

T F 3. Today's refrigerators consume half the energy of those sold a decade ago.

T F 4. Most of the world's original forest cover has been taken down.

T F 5. In all less developed countries, birth rates continue to rise.

T F 6. The British government's plan for achieving sustainable development includes an emphasis on promoting personal well-being and social health.

T F 7. Half the world's people live on less than two dollars a day.

T F 8. Research indicates that Scandinavians are happier than Bulgarians.

T F 9. One route to a sustainable future is through increasing technological efficiency and agricultural productivity.

T F 10. Research suggests that people who strive for intrinsic goals such as intimacy, personal growth, and contribution to community experience a higher quality of life.

T F 11. To reduce consumption, Robert Frank proposes that we tax people on what they spend rather than on what they earn.

T F 12. Research suggests that individuals who strive most for wealth tend to experience a lower level of well-being.

T F 13. Since 1957 the American divorce rate has doubled and the teen suicide rate has more than doubled.

T F 14. According to one Gallup Poll, 4 in 5 Americans earning more than $75,000 say that they would like to be rich.

T F 15. About 40 percent of Americans worry a great deal about global warming.

T F 16. American college students now rank "raising a family" as their number one objective.

T F 17. In both the United States and Britain, the correlation between income and personal happiness is weak.

T　F　18.　Very rich people are significantly happier than the average person.

T　F　19.　Americans reporting themselves "very happy" has declined slightly since 1957.

T　F　20.　Economic growth in affluent societies has provided no apparent boost to human morale.

T　F　21.　The adaptation-level phenomenon suggests that we can learn to adjust to a simplified way of living.

T　F　22.　People have little difficulty predicting the intensity and duration of their future positive and negative emotions.

T　F　23.　Optimism, self-esteem, perceived control, and extroversion are all predictive of greater well-being.

T　F　24.　Compared to those who never attend, those who attend religious services regularly are less likely to declare themselves as being very happy.

T　F　25.　Most people are happier gardening than power boating.

MULTIPLE-CHOICE PRACTICE TEST

Circle the correct letter.

1.　Which of the following statements regarding the challenge of global warming is true?

   a.　There is strong scientific evidence that global warming is occurring and that it poses a significant threat to human well-being
   b.　Scientists are divided on whether global warming is occurring
   c.　Scientists agree that global warming is occurring but disagree on whether it poses a significant threat to human welfare
   d.　Scientists believe that although global warming has been occurring it is less of a threat today than it was a decade ago

2.　Studies of world population indicate that

   a.　all countries will show an increase in population between now and 2050
   b.　nearly all of the population increase between now and 2050 is expected in the world's poorest countries
   c.　only ten countries will lose population between now and 2050
   d.　birth rates continue to increase in all less developed countries

3. Studies of population growth and consumption indicate that today Earth has

   a. 8.4 billion people and 7 million restaurants
   b. 12.2 billion people and 500 million factories
   c. 3.6 billion people and 700 nuclear power plants
   d. 6.6 billion people and 500 million cars

4. The United States accounts for _____ percent of the world's population but consumes _____ percent of the world's energy.

   a. 3; 62   c. 5; 26
   b. 11; 52   d. 9; 18

5. The text suggests that plausible future technologies include

   a. cars that run on water
   b. washing machines that consume no water, heat, or soap
   c. edible plants that require no nutrients to grow
   d. shoes and clothes that never show wear

6. If birth rates everywhere immediately fell to replacement levels,

   a. population growth would also immediately stop
   b. total population would immediately begin a slow decline
   c. total population would immediately begin a rapid decline
   d. population growth would still continue for years to come

7. Birth rates have fallen where

   a. food security has improved and women have become educated and empowered
   b. employment has increased and inflation has decreased
   c. food prices have stabilized and hard liquor consumption has been controlled
   d. males are better educated and materialism declines

8. Economist Robert Frank proposes that we reduce consumption by taxing people on what they

   a. sell   c. spend
   b. earn   d. weigh

9. Research suggests that those who strive most for _____ tend to live with lower well-being.

   a. autonomy   c. wealth
   b. relatedness   d. self-esteem

10. Since 1957, American life was marked by an increase in

    a.   teen suicide
    b.   mental health
    c.   happiness
    d.   charitable contributions

11. Survey research indicates that _____ percent of Americans worry "a great deal" about global warming.

    a.   12
    b.   28
    c.   52
    d.   74

12. According to the text, what constitutes the "American paradox"?

    a.   soaring wealth and a shrinking spirit
    b.   increased volunteerism and increased violence
    c.   improved standard of living and decreased longevity
    d.   increased concern for diversity and an increased number of hate crimes

13. New American collegians rank _____ as their number one objective.

    a.   becoming very well-off financially
    b.   developing a meaningful philosophy of life
    c.   helping others in difficulty
    d.   raising a family

14. Research on national wealth and well-being indicates that

    a.   the Bulgarians are happier than the Irish
    b.   in poor countries, such as India, being relatively well off does not predict greater well-being
    c.   the Swiss and the Scandinavians are generally prosperous but unhappy
    d.   in affluent societies, where most can afford life's necessities, affluence shows very little relationship to personal happiness

15. A survey of the *Forbes* 100 wealthiest Americans found that they are _____ happy than average.

    a.   significantly more
    b.   slightly more
    c.   slightly less
    d.   significantly less

16. Since 1957 Americans' inflation-adjusted income has doubled. Since 1957 the number of Americans reporting themselves "very happy"

    a.   increased dramatically
    b.   increased moderately
    c.   increased slightly
    d.   decreased slightly

17. Research indicates that since 1957 the rate of _____ in the United State has doubled.

    a. church attendance
    b. homicide
    c. schizophrenia
    d. divorce

18. Research involving university students indicates that the most personally satisfying events are those associated with a need for

    a. wealth
    b. autonomy
    c. beauty
    d. popularity

19. The two principles that help explain why people are not happier after attaining greater wealth are

    a. flow and social comparison
    b. Parkinson's second law and flow
    c. the adaptation-level phenomenon and social comparison
    d. the adaptation-level phenomenon and displacement

20. The tendency to adapt to a given level of stimulation and thus to notice and react to changes from that level is

    a. relative deprivation
    b. ecological footprints
    c. the adaptation-level phenomenon
    d. Parkinson's second law

21. Our tendency for social comparison frequently results in

    a. the adaptation-level phenomenon
    b. relative deprivation
    c. flow
    d. communal "we" thinking

22. Tim Kasser reports that those who strive for _____ experience a higher quality of life.

    a. personal growth
    b. safety
    c. social recognition
    d. beauty

23. Ed Diener and his colleagues report that people who identify with expensive possessions experience fewer

    a. depressive episodes
    b. symptoms of physical illness
    c. positive moods
    d. failed romances

24. After a baseball player signs for $12 million a year, a $7 million teammate who has equal skill is most likely to experience

   a. flow
   b. relative deprivation
   c. reaction formation
   d. projection

25. The difficult people have in predicting the intensity and duration of their future emotions is called _____ bias.

   a. adaptation
   b. self-serving
   c. comparison
   d. impact

26. Marshall Dermer found that after women imagined and wrote about being burned and disfigured they

   a. became deeply depressed
   b. were more responsive to a request for help
   c. expressed greater satisfaction with their own lives
   d. experienced a significant loss in personal control

27. Csikszentmihalyi reports that people are most likely to experience flow when

   a. unself-consciously absorbed in a mindful challenge
   b. involved in a passive leisure activity that requires little thought
   c. involved in intense interpersonal conflict with a close relative
   d. passing from the state of wakefulness to sleep

28. Most people are happier when _____ than when _____.

   a. gardening; power boating
   b. power boating; gardening
   c. watching TV; talking to friends
   d. watching TV; power boating

29. According to the text, people are much likelier to declare themselves "very happy" if they

   a. are highly educated
   b. have intimate friendships
   c. are physically attractive
   d. have many children

30. In comparison to those who never attend religious services, those who attend weekly are more likely to declare themselves

   a. very happy
   b. depressed
   c. pessimistic
   d. shy

31. Which personal trait has been positively related to happiness?

    a. self-esteem   c. instability
    b. introversion   d. passivity

32. When first-year university students predicted their satisfaction with various housing possibilities shortly before entering their school's housing lottery, they focused on _____ features.

    a. physical   c. psychological
    b. social   d. spiritual

33. Economic growth and increased consumption have been accompanied by increases in

    a. the polar ice caps   c. forest cover
    b. air temperature   d. stocks of wild salmon and herring

34. Joanna is certain that if she wins the super lottery her level of happiness will be significantly higher for the rest of her life. Joanna is apparently unaware of

    a. the self-serving bias   c. the fundamental attribution error
    b. framing effects   d. the impact bias

35. Jennifer Crocker and Lisa Gallo reported that people who five times completed the sentence "I'm glad I'm not a…" afterward felt

    a. greater relative deprivation and stress in their lives
    b. greater prejudice toward minority groups
    c. less depressed and more satisfied with their lives
    d. less purpose in life and greater uncertainty about the direction of their lives

36. A 65-degree day seems warm in February but cold in July. This is best explained in terms of

    a. relative deprivation   c. displacement
    b. the adaptation-level phenomenon   d. Parkinson's second law

37. After Tim won one million dollars in the state lottery, he was ecstatic. After a year, however, his sense of life satisfaction returned to what it was before he won. This change in Tim's feelings can best be explained in terms of

    a. social comparison   c. the adaptation-level phenomenon
    b. flow   d. opponent-process theory

38. Tawanna was happy with her grade of C on her social psychology test until she learned that all her classmates received As or Bs. The shift in Tawanna's feelings is best explained in terms of

   a. Parkinson's second law
   b. the adaptation-level phenomeon
   c. reaction formation
   d. social comparison

39. Hong's leisure activities include watching television, woodcarving, power boating, and sitting alone in the woods. Research suggest he is most likely to experience "flow" when

   a. daydreaming in the woods
   b. power boating
   c. woodcarving
   d. watching television

40. Michelle is a saleswoman who is depressed because recently she was denied a promotion. To increase her happiness with life, Michelle should

   a. imagine what her life would be like if she received a paralyzing physical injury
   b. compare her life with the co-worker who actually received the promotion
   c. recall moments from her early childhood when she was very happy
   d. identify the negative qualities of her supervisor who denied the promotion

SHORT ESSAY QUESTIONS

Answer the following questions in the space provided.

1. Briefly describe the nature of the present global crisis.

2. Discuss two different routes to sustainable lifestyles.

3. Discuss the relationship between wealth and well-being.

4. Briefly explain the adaptation-level phenomenon and the process of social comparison.

5. Identify the factors that seem to be associated with a genuinely good life.

ANSWER KEY

Chapter Review

1. best
    population
    consumption
    pollution
    warming
    destruction

2. efficiency
    consumption
    spend
    earn
    incentives
    penalties

3. increased
    first
    well-being
    well-being
    weak
    rich
    no

4. wealth
    relatedness

5. adaptation
    stimulation

6. comparison
    upward

7. downward
    comparison

8. close
    communities
    thinking
    flow

Matching Terms

1. d	6. b
2. f	7. i
3. g	8. c
4. h	9. a
5. e	

True-False Review

1. F	14. T
2. T	15. F
3. T	16. F
4. T	17. T
5. F	18. F
6. T	19. T
7. T	20. T
8. T	21. T
9. T	22. F
10. T	23. T
11. T	24. F
12. T	25. T
13. T	

Multiple-Choice Practice Test

1. a	21. b
2. b	22. a
3. d	23. c
4. c	24. b
5. b	25. d
6. d	26. c
7. a	27. a
8. c	28. a
9. c	29. b
10. a	30. a
11. b	31. a
12. a	32. a
13. a	33. b
14. d	34. d
15. b	35. c
16. d	36. b
17. d	37. c
18. b	38. d
19. c	39. c
20. c	40. a